Turning the Self Inside Out

A Self-Discovery Guide for Gen Y

by

Richard Longworth

iUniverse, Inc.
New York Bloomington

Turning the Self Inside Out
A Self-Discovery Guidebook for Gen Y

Copyright © 2009 by Richard Longworth

All rights reserved. No part of this book may be reproduced, copied, stored, or transmitted in any form or by any means without prior written permission from the author, except where permitted by law.

The information contained in this book is intended for information purposes only and not for diagnosis, prescription, or treatment of any health disorder whatsoever. The author is in no way liable for any misuse of the material.

iUniverse books may be ordered through booksellers or by contacting:

iUniverse
1663 Liberty Drive
Bloomington, IN 47403
www.iuniverse.com
1-800-Authors (1-800-288-4677)

Because of the dynamic nature of the Internet, any Web addresses or links contained in this book may have changed since publication and may no longer be valid. The views expressed in this work are solely those of the author and do not necessarily reflect the views of the publisher, and the publisher hereby disclaims any responsibility for them.

ISBN: 978-0-595-50019-2 (pbk)
ISBN: 978-0-595-61344-1 (ebk)

Printed in the United States of America

iUniverse rev. date: 1/6/09

Dedication

To all who are seeking to effect change

Contents

Author's Note	xi
Introduction	xiii
Prologue	xix
Chapter 1 Abundance	1
Chapter 2 Completeness	7
Chapter 3 Presence	13
Chapter 4 Intention	19
Chapter 5 Reality	26
Chapter 6 Effort	33
Chapter 7 Learning	39
Chapter 8 Control	45

Chapter 9	
Time	50
Chapter 10	
Health	56
Chapter 11	
Relationships	63
Chapter 12	
Self-Actualization	69
Chapter 13	
Taking Stock	76
Chapter 14	
The New You	79
Chapter 15	
So What's Next?	87
Appendices	93
Notes	111
Resources	115
Bibliography	117

Acknowledgments

Grateful appreciation to: my family, friends, students, and colleagues for their words of encouragement, invaluable input, patience, and guidance during the creation of this book.

In particular, to: Ann Anchor, Pat Buckna, John Cotling, Frank Harris, Doug Loblaw, Sandy Molendyk, George Nikolov, Barbara Stechysin, and Bethany Tapp, who deserve more recognition than a simple thank-you—without their contributions, the task would have been impossible to complete.

And very special thanks to my wife, Glenda, who recognized the importance of our counseling and teachings, and persuaded me to tell our story.

Author's Note

I have spent the last forty years working voluntarily with youth groups and teaching in a community college. I always considered helping young people to be my primary career goal, and teaching and training to be my secondary goal. Early in my career, I realized that I could separate my work into two distinct parts: a "doing" structured part, and a "being" unstructured part. Initially, I concentrated my effort on the "doing" part, but eventually I realized that the "being" part was far more important than the "doing." Time and time again, when I asked my students which of their instructors had a significant effect on their life, most identified the teacher who could reach out and connect with them on a human level, not the teacher who had subject-matter expertise or delivered an effective lecture. Good teaching comes from the heart and not the mind.

When questioned about their reason for teaching, instructors will frequently articulate a philosophy of education based on discussions at teaching college or dictated by an education ministry. Whether this educational philosophy is essentialism or perennialism or progressivism, most teachers identify a specific content and structure as their basis for teaching and student learning. Unfortunately, very few emphasize the essence of teaching. Parker Palmer documented this in his landmark book, *The Courage to Teach.* He suggests that too much emphasis is placed on the whats and hows (content and structure) of teaching: "What topic shall we teach? How shall I structure the lesson? And rarely, if ever, do we ask the important who question (essence): Who is the self that teaches?"[1] If we accept the premise that the teacher who can connect with the student has a significant effect on the learner, then it follows that the teacher needs to ask how (s)he can teach from the heart—for the sake of the learner.

This book is not about a new philosophy of education, although there are strong hints of one. Nor is this book intended for teachers, though it may provide some insight into the essence of teaching. Instead, this book, though directed primarily to Generation Y, has a message for all of us. It is about who we are, how we think and learn, how we experience life, and why we need to change. The message has the potential for turning the self inside out.

Introduction

We are at a point in human history when there is an urgent need for change. The old ways are just not working. Many of our current problems seem to be repeats from the past. At best, these issues are systematic; at worst, they are acute. Either way, there are too many apparently unsolvable issues. We have global problems involving crime, hostility, culture and religion, security, terrorism, overpopulation, poverty, global warming, the environment, pollution. Even our youth have their issues. College students face an alarming number of worries, including pressures of school, social acceptance, drugs, relationships, physical appearance, gangs, peer pressure, student loans, even information overload. These stresses produce a state of anxiety, stress, and depression in some of our young. These types of issues have arguably been around in the past. Unfortunately, though, they keep reappearing.

In general, when faced with insurmountable problems in the past, we took the time and invested financial resources to cope and make necessary changes. The recurring issues not only continue to require these resources but also demand our urgent attention. We need to reengineer our thinking in order to solve these problems. Otherwise we may engineer our demise.

Ken Wilber remarks that, whatever the process of evolution was, it seems to have an incredible intelligence—from matter to life to mind to conscious awareness. But it is strange that the very mechanisms that allowed evolution to become conscious of itself were simultaneously working to engineer its own extinction.[1]

Our conceptualization of reality is based on seeing things from the outside and translating what we see with our intellectual mind—a sort of myopic, limited, one-self view of reality. The corrective vision we need is primarily to see reality from the inside and then tap into the outside universal intelligence.

Is this new view possible? The corrective lenses are available and await our use. Our shortsightedness is now so severe that we need to take action. My fear is that we will continue with the old prescription and repeat the same errors that have plagued us for eons.

This book should appeal to all age groups; the content, however, is directed mostly to the young person. I believe this is important because young people need to have a solid understanding of conscious awareness. Why is this? Our parents, the school system, the work environment, and society instill in us a sense of what is right and wrong. Even what we read in the newspaper and magazines and on the Internet is an affirmation of societal norms. Young people are unaware of the effect this has on their psyches. They are not taught consciously to decide whether something is correct or incorrect. In most cases, our experience of our experiences is influenced by whether our responses match the established norm. "What is right?" we ask. We rely mostly on our conditioning and end up never finding who we really are. To paraphrase Ken Wilbur in his book, *Sex, Ecology, Spirituality:* The very mechanisms that allowed evolution to become conscious of itself were never taught how to use this new intelligence; instead, the gatekeepers continued teaching and preaching the old intellectual paradigm that simply maintained the existing system. It is far easier to continue with the old patterns: they are effective, and those in charge were taught in the same manner. There is little interest in the system to delve into a new reality—conscious awareness. But the time has come to change the old and bring in the new. Conversations with young people suggest that they have come to a realization that a new view of what is real is necessary. Believing this, I am optimistic that not only are today's young adults our hope for a better tomorrow, but also that they have the potential to effect change. Herein is the purpose of this book. It is written to help guide Gen Y in achieving a new vision.

The book identifies twelve paradigms and their significance for Generation Y. The choice of the paradigms was quite arbitrary, since I could have selected others, but I felt that these twelve are important reality checks, although restricted to a particular perspective: abundance (limited/unlimited potential), completeness (separation/wholeness), presence (past or future/present moment), intention (doing/being), reality (beliefs/truths), effort (struggle/effortless), learning (resistance/acceptance), control (mind problems/mind control), time (time-bound/timelessness), health (negative/positive thinking), relationships (share conditionally/give unconditionally), and self-actualization (limited/complete awareness).

This is not a "once upon a time" book with a sequence of story events. It simply unfolds as life itself unfolds. The book begins here and ends where you take it. Chapter 1 plunges right away into the first paradigm. Perhaps you have a general plan outlining where you are going in life, but from moment to moment there is little in the way of a plan. This book is about the here and now, and how you can deal with it effectively. The first nine chapters lay out some concepts; chapters ten through twelve apply these concepts; and the last three chapters sum up, conclude, and look to the future. There is no actual end to this book. The end belongs to you. You design and develop the finished product like a new creation. As you work through the book, I hope you experience some "aha" moments, some clarity of thought. Within the pages of the book a number of gems are buried, but you must discover their relevance for your own life, and use them to your best advantage.

The following is a sampling of questions and issues that will be addressed:

- What is the cause of most of our life problems? *Chapter 1*
- How can we reengineer our thinking and solve many of these life problems? *Chapter 1*
- Why do we have little control over what we are thinking? *Chapters 1 and 8*
- How can we take control of our thoughts? *Chapter 2*
- How can we become interconnected with the whole of humanity? *Chapter 2*
- How can negative thoughts and feelings become positive? *Chapters 1, 2, and 10*
- Why is the present moment so important? *Chapters 3, 9, and 14*
- What is the optimal level for lifelong learning? *Chapters 4 and 7*
- What is a "being" person? *Chapters 4 and 8*
- Why is reality an illusion? *Chapter 5*
- How can we find joy and happiness? *Chapters 6 and 12*
- How can we live a healthy life? *Chapter 10*
- How can we develop strong relationships? *Chapter 11*

- Why is meditation so beneficial for our mind, body, and soul? *Chapter 14*

- What is the purpose of life? *Chapter 15*

This resource guide is practical, hands-on, engaging, and interactive. At the end of each of the first twelve chapters, readers are asked to reflect on the concepts that were presented (What Does This Have to Do with Me); to validate, based on their own experience, what they learned (Reality Check); and to research questions through additional resources, and to interact with other readers at the author's Web site (Things to Try). The last three chapters apply the knowledge gained from the previous chapters and look at sustainable life issues of health, relationships, and self-fulfillment.

Turning the Self Inside Out is a work of the heart. My hope is that the book will have some meaning for you and possibly be an inspiration that will lead you toward a better future.

Prologue

Our journey of self-discovery is woven into twelve arbitrary paradigms. A paradigm describes a concept acceptable to most people in an intellectual community.[1] When a paradigm becomes subconscious, it defines its own reality based on personal experience and becomes very difficult to replace. Einstein suggests that "Many insoluble problems have no solution until either the paradigm or the consciousness that created the problem is changed." I will discuss each one of the twelve paradigms in the book in the context of two mind-sets: the old and the new; the limited and the universal mind-set (adopted in this book). A limited or old mind-set is our normal way of viewing reality—that is, from the outside in. Psychology tells us that we experience external stimuli and then react based on our memory. Our reaction is therefore limited to our past knowledge. This is the primary source of our problems. A universal mind-set is a view from the inside out. This new mind-set can be thought of as a paradigm shift. If we did not rely on our memory or past experience, how would we react? Would we not judge an experience in its purest sense?

There is an overarching paradigm (the principal paradigm) with which the reader should become familiar in advance. It is the notion of conscious awareness. This principal paradigm is contained within each of the twelve paradigms. Ken Wilbur was not the first to mention that humans have a unique awareness of the self. The original concept was first presented by John Locke in his work *An Essay Concerning Human Understanding*. John Locke, however, never used the phrase conscious awareness but instead spoke of personal identity. Later, the French philosopher Jean-Paul Sartre coined the phrase conscious awareness in his treatise *Being and Nothingness* (1943). More recently, the concept of conscious awareness has been rooted in quantum physics, neuroscience, the cognitive sciences, and extensions of philosophy and psychology.

A chapter is devoted to each of the paradigms. To gain maximum value, read each chapter slowly; stop at various points to allow the concepts to percolate. Some of the ideas need to be thought out carefully. After reading a chapter in its entirety and completing the exercise questions, take a breather, and return to the book at a later time.

Chapter 1

Abundance
Limited/Unlimited Potential

A beggar had been sitting by the side of the road for over thirty years. One day a stranger walked by. "Spare some change?" mumbled the beggar, mechanically holding out his old baseball cap. "I have nothing to give you," said the stranger. Then he asked, "What's that you are sitting on?" "Nothing," replied the beggar. "Just an old box. I have been sitting on it for as long as I can remember." "Ever looked inside?" asked the stranger. "No," said the beggar. "What's the point? There's nothing in there." "Have a look inside," insisted the stranger. The beggar managed to pry open the lid. With astonishment, disbelief, and elation, he saw that the box was filled with gold.

—Eckhart Tolle, *The Power of Now*

We seem to be destined to do things the same way as every other person. Rarely do we look beyond the reality that is in front of us.

As in the epigraph above, if we could only look within, we would probably find a priceless treasure. If we could uncover the inner self and work from the inside out, we would discover not only abundance, but also a life filled with joy and serenity. Amazingly, we would see things differently and thus discover a potential of unlimited opportunity.

How can you plug into this bountiful wealth? The first step is simply to try to become more aware of what is happening around you, but with a different mind-set. This new mind-set does not make prior judgment of situations, nor does it attach labels to objects or allow the intellectual mind to interfere. This new mind-set simply observes with pure awareness. Let us investigate this phenomenon more closely.

Here is a hypothetical situation using the old mind-set:

While observing your body, you notice the pain in your back. "Poor me, I've had this pain far too long. When are the doctors going to find out what's wrong? They must be stupid. My friends just don't realize the pain I am going through. Why is this happening to me?" On and on and on. This dialogue is with the mind and is typical of our thinking process. The mind has shifted the responsibility of the pain to doctors and friends who fail to understand our problem. Blaming other people does not help the problem. Why, then, allow the mind to engage in a negative discourse with itself? As in the case of the beggar, far better to take a different approach. We need to circumvent our thinking mind, since most thoughts are similar: negative, blaming others, judgmental. Instead, we need a mind-set that is free from negative thoughts and is limitless in its potential.

How can you change this situation using the new mind-set?

You need to begin by taking control of your mind. Observe your thoughts—look within. If you focus directly on what the mind is saying, the negative dialogue will stop. In later chapters, techniques will be provided on how to take control of the mind. Horse trainers understand the importance of taking control with a light touch of the reins. Similarly, you will learn how a gentle nudge will stop the mind from wandering off. Perhaps not immediately, but you will eventually gain control. Buddha said, "There is nothing so obedient as a disciplined mind, and nothing more disobedient as an undisciplined mind."[1]

Another scenario (old mind-set):

Do you sometimes say to other people, perhaps a boy or girlfriend, "You take me for granted; you don't appreciate me. I am giving so much and you so little. I always do what you want. You never do what I want." The statement may or may not be true, but this is surely a script for a heated dialogue. Can you imagine the emotional response from the other person?

Enter the new mind-set:

Your perception of the relationship is that you are not receiving what you deserve. Perhaps you feel you are not receiving appreciation, attention, positive feedback, maybe love. Other concepts that the intellectual mind dwells on are lack of money, success, time. To change this, go beyond the old mind-set, and work from within. Give what you think you are lacking with all your heart. The mind makes it so easy to say or do things, but giving from the heart is an entirely different matter. In the words of Mother Teresa: "It is not how much we do, but how much love we put into the doing. And it is not how much we give, but how much love we put into the giving."[2]

In psychology, it is a well-known fact that what you are lacking, you fail to give. Test it out. Whatever you think the other person is not giving to you, give it to them: utmost attention, unconditional love, unlimited time, even money. In return, you will receive what you desire, and a limitless abundance will flow into your life.

What Does This Have to Do with Me?

How can a simple change in our mind-set lead to untold wealth? The old mind-set pays little or no attention to what is happening around us. The new mind-set is observing with full awareness and attention. Practically, what can we expect from this switch in mind-sets? Carl Rogers, who worked in psychotherapy for over forty years, claimed it would "enhance interpersonal relationships, enable you to become an effective decision-maker, empower you to take more control of your life, ensure recognition for who you are, ensure success in everything that you try, lead a path toward happiness, and much much more."[3]

Reality Check

For each statement below, give a rating from 1 to 5 as follows: 1 strongly agree, 2 somewhat agree, 3 neutral, 4 disagree, 5 strongly disagree.

Statement	Rating
1. Do you believe that your IQ, previous academic history, even your teacher determine how well you do in school?	_____
2. Is your genetic makeup a determination of your future success?	_____
3. Do you believe in bad karma?	_____
4. Do you believe that you have little control of your thoughts?	_____
Score (add up the numbers in the rating column, and write the sum)	_____

Interpretation

The maximum possible score is twenty. The lower the sum, the more your mind-set needs to plug into the universal wavelength. The higher the value, the greater the possibility that you are attuned to the new paradigm. But don't despair; a value much below twenty only indicates that you are not convinced, and if you find the paradigm shift intriguing, attempt the "Things to Try" below.

Things to Try

If your daily life is filled with happiness and you find joy in what you do, then it is not necessary to make any changes. If you would like to investigate further, however, try the following:

1. Turn to Appendix B at the back of this book. Complete the questions, and find your ranking.

Chapter 2

Completeness
Separation/Wholeness

Imagine this: your big toe complains that it has no room to move when you are wearing a pair of tight shoes. It looks over at the little toe and says, "Look at all the room you have. I'm big toe. Why should you have more space than I? Just wait till I get the chance—I'm going to squeeze you out and show you what it's like to be hurting." Big toe is isolating itself and does not comprehend its relationship to the whole.

How absurd. Doesn't any hurt to the big toe affect the whole foot? Similarly, isn't a black or brown or white person part of the whole of humanity? People may differ on the surface. People have different religious beliefs and cultural views. These differences are slight, like the differences between toes. Essentially we are all the same. Albert Einstein wrote: "A human being is part of the whole, called by us the Universe, a part limited in space and time. He experiences himself, his thoughts and feelings as something separated from the rest—a kind of optical delusion of his consciousness. This delusion is a prison for us. Our task must be to free ourselves from this prison by widening our circle of compassion to embrace all living creatures and the whole of nature in its beauty."[1]

Personal Reflections

Just recently, I spoke with a graduate from our business department. He was upset because he was stuck in a career that was leading nowhere. "What should I do?" "Is there a better choice for me?" were two of his questions. He could change his job and try a different one. He might, however, go from one job to another and still not be satisfied. Possibly his problem was caused by the way he sees and thinks about things, an "optical delusion." Is this graduate being true to himself? Should he look at the bigger picture? Perhaps he should look more closely at the source of his dissatisfaction rather than at just one particular situation.

The mind, by its very nature and structure, divides issues into separate problems, trying to find an answer through its own thinking process. If we observe carefully, we find that the mind divides and compartmentalizes our problems into neat packages, where each problem is considered separate from any other problem. The mind then tries to solve the separate problem without any regard to the whole.

Some days we are upset over something that has happened. For example, we just do not feel like leaving the house, going to school, or even talking to other people. Some root cause affects our moods.

Perhaps the cause of this feeling was a criticism from a friend who said, "I don't like you sharing our secret with your brother after we agreed not to tell anyone." An isolated event may affect our whole view of life.

On a larger scale, we, as a society, try to solve our problems by isolating them. Violence, vandalism, drugs, and prostitution are interrelated, but we try to solve them by forming different groups like MADD, AA, Vandal Watch. The various groups try to solve each problem as if it was separate from the rest.

What Does This Have to Do with Me?

As we go through life, we face innumerable problems. Our normal response is to worry, and focus all our attention on our individual problems. Do you find that, whenever you have an unresolved or perceived problem, it tends to magnify, and eventually becomes a continuous, nagging thought throughout your day? The specific problem is often a separate issue, usually unconnected to our daily undertakings, but it plays havoc with our emotional psyche. Like the big toe, which considers itself to be separate, our free-flowing, isolated thoughts dominate our mind-set when a problem arises.

Now that we are more aware of the impact that problems have on daily existence, we can take a proactive approach and react with a conscious mind-set. Since any part affects the whole, we come to the realization that our perception and reaction to a problem can ripple beyond us. If we believe that our thoughts and feelings are something unique, we delude ourselves into believing that we are separate from humanity. If we view our problems holistically, however, we can change our view and become better connected with the rest of society.

How do we integrate a holistic approach into our lives? By looking at the whole, and not just one aspect of the problem. Consider the situation in which we harbor an ill thought toward another person. Through gossip, it can easily ripple through our family, with others that we communicate with, and even much further. We are all interrelated, and we need to be aware of how one thought can propagate into the whole of society.

More globally, when assessing the potential health effects of toxic wastes from industry, we need to look at the impact not just on human life, but also on the environment. What is the result of such a holistic approach? A sense of conscious awareness; a clearer understanding of the impact of our thoughts; a belief that our action is right for a given situation; a strong alignment with the whole of life. Edgar Mitchell, an astronaut, must have experienced this as he approached the planet that we know as home: "He was filled with an inner conviction as certain as any mathematical equation he'd ever solved. He knew that the beautiful blue world to which he was returning is part of a living system, harmonious and whole—and that we all participate, in a universe of consciousness."[2]

Reality Check

For each statement below, answer "yes" or "no" under the rating column. Give some thought to the additional "If so" questions in Statements 3 and 4.

Statement	Rating
1. Based on what has been presented in this chapter, do you agree with the statement that "The whole is greater than the sum of the parts?"	_____
2. Do you believe that thoughts can create emotions?	_____
3. Based on what was presented in this chapter, do you believe that some advocacy groups are doing the right thing? If so, try to identify what they do and why they are successful.	_____
4. When we think of the field of psychiatry, we envision a therapist who listens intently, provides feedback, but offers little in the way of solving a problem. Do you agree with this statement? If so, why do you think psychiatrists act this way?	_____
Score (add up the "yes" answers, and write the sum)	_____

Interpretation

We are looking for "yes" answers to each of the questions above. Try to write answers for the "If so" questions above.

Things to Try

1. Reread the scenario about the business student trying to find the right job. Write an answer, either for yourself or in answer to the student's question, and post your response on the blog at: http://turningselfinsideout.blogspot.com/ under Chapter 2 (see Appendix A).

2. Each night, revisit your day. Do a playback of the major events that took place that day. For each event, ask yourself whether there were any negative feelings. If so, change your view of the event until it produces a positive feeling. For example, in the scenario above where the gal told a secret to her brother, change your understanding of the incident to give it a positive spin.

3. Take an interest in some issue that appears in a magazine or newspaper. If you have a view based on a holistic approach, write a scenario on how you would solve the issue. Either store your response for future reference, or better, send it as a news item to turningselfinsideout@gmail.com.

Chapter 3

Presence
Living in the Past or Future/
Living the Present Moment

This is a story of two monks, Tanzan and Ekido, who were walking along a muddy road after a torrential downpour. Near a village, they came across a young woman who was having difficulty crossing the road. The mud was deep, and she was too small to cross safely. Tanzan at once picked her up and carried her to the other side. Five hours later Ekido asked of his friend, "Why did you carry that girl across the road? We monks are not allowed to do things like that." Tanzan replied, "I put the girl down five hours ago; are you still carrying her?"

—based on a story by the Japanese Zen master Tanzan

This chapter discusses the possibility of giving our complete attention to the present moment. In our present state, we fear the future: "Will

I have enough money? Have I selected the right career? Will my health fail me?" We also worry about the past: "If only I had realized the importance of a good education, saved for the future, bought a house instead of renting." We fill our lives with fear, doubt, worries. Our normal tendencies are psychotic, a delusion of reality brought on by a mind-set that continually escapes from the here and now. Like Tanzan, let go of all heavy burdens from the past, dismiss any thoughts that negatively affect you. Further, avoid what-if concerns that are out of your control: "What if the plane crashes?" "What if I lose my job?" The future will always present itself at some later date, and, in most cases, differently from how we envision it today.

With our intelligence, we should be able to rid ourselves of the worries that fester within us—the dramas that are played out and magnified in our minds. "Be gone, and don't bother me anymore" is what we need to say, and yet the doubts and fears return again and again. Wouldn't it be wonderful if we were able to control our thinking, understand what is taking place inside of us, and fend off all our worries?

Why are we unable to do this? Quite possibly, we fail to recognize an intelligence that is within each one of us. Instead, we turn to others and expect them to help us. How often do we hear: "Don't worry; tomorrow will be a better day. Take it a day at a time. You'll live through it. It's really not so bad." Do these statements eradicate our doubts and fears? Unfortunately not. Our impression is that others either have no interest or are unable to help us. Instead, we need to take responsibility for negative feelings that we created in the past or imagine in the future. Doubts and fears will simply disappear if we are to free our minds and immerse ourselves in the present moment. How are we to do this? The following personal experience might help.

Personal Reflections

My work with youth groups included crisis intervention. During this time, there was a horrible situation where one of the teens phoned me and told me he was at a railway crossing contemplating suicide. After some negotiation, I convinced him to reconsider what he was doing, and we agreed that we needed some time together. His concerns centered on his past failures—many of them typical teenager worries (not to trivialize the conversations we had over the next week). It would have been easy to say, "Don't be so worried. You are no different from most teens," or, "Grow up, and get your life under control." This, however, would merely have dismissed his experiences and been of little help to him. Instead, we considered a change of mind-set. "If I had a magic wand," I told him, "and was able to erase all your past experiences, how would you feel right now?" He thought about it and said, "Probably all right." "Do you believe that the bird on the tree above us, the ladybug we see on the leaf, and the butterfly over there are worried about their past?" "Well, no," he remarked. "They probably have little, if any, recollection of their past." I then asked, "Would you say they are in a better state of being?" His short reply was, "Yes." "By that admission, you have just suggested that thinking about the past is harmful to you," I told him. "And why not use your supreme intelligence and choose not to dwell on previous damaging events. We all have this choice, every moment, every day."

What Does This Have to Do with Me?

Do you find yourself in a situation where you are worried? For example, you find you don't have enough money to pay the tuition fees for the upcoming semester. You phone a friend who responds with a typical, "Don't worry. You'll sort it out." You watch your favorite reality show on TV, a sort of escape. Not much help here, and the problem returns once the TV program is over. Your mind starts talking to you, "You'll be kicked out of school, and you will have to take a meaningless job. What a failure you are." The problem overwhelms you. It takes over your life. The problem is now a serious concern.

This scenario is all too familiar. The mind, in its normal state, is not helping. In fact, it is doing grievous damage. The first thing you need to do is recognize what is actually taking place and take some positive action. You need damage control. Be aware that you have lost focus by allowing the mind to concentrate on the future. The focal point of the mind must be on the present moment. By concentrating on the present moment, all worries and doubts will take their place in line and not be a burden to you, the thinker. A new energy source will replace the worry, and you will find creative solutions to your problems.

Here is an approach to concentrating on the present moment, a technique that you can practice with all routine tasks. As an example, let's assume you are washing the dishes. While washing the dishes, say to yourself, "Here I am, washing dishes." Repeat it calmly to yourself and continue to focus on the task of washing the dishes. Next, as you continue with the dishes, be aware of the water running out of the tap, the soap floating on top of the water, the smell of the soap, the soapy water that runs off a dish, etc. The purpose of this is to concentrate only on the present moment. Very quickly, you will feel relaxed. You let go of the past and future. Other events lose importance. You are giving direct orders to the mind to focus on what you are doing right now.

Try the technique with other tasks that you perform on a regular basis. You will find release—even a surge of new energy, a sense of well-being. The stresses and worries that were prevalent earlier will suddenly disappear.

Reality Check

For statements 1 and 2 below, record under the rating column the number of times each event occurred.

Statement	Rating
1. During a class lecture, count how many times, over two minutes, your mind wanders off?	_____
2. Sit quietly by yourself, close your eyes, and, over a two-minute period, check off the number of times that a thought enters your mind.	_____
3. Try to recognize your feelings by asking yourself at different times during the day, "How am I feeling today?" "Am I experiencing a good feeling or a bad feeling?"	_____
4. Make a three-column list, one column with a heading that reads "negative," a second column that reads "positive," and a third column that reads "neutral." Stop what you are doing at different times during the day, and identify what you are thinking by ticking off one of the columns.*	_____

*Research indicates that, on average, 77 percent of the population thinks negative thoughts.[1]

Interpretation

Asking the above questions is a simple means of connecting with your thoughts. You may be surprised by the results. Ask yourself, "Am I really concentrating on what is being said?" Even your quiet moments are noisy times for the mind. How you presently feel is an indicator of your thought pattern.

Things to Try

Summarize in your own words what you learned by answering the questions in the Reality Check above. It is important that the words you use have a positive or neutral spin. For example, write, "I will make a concentrated effort to listen to the lecture presentation."

1. Now that you have gained some insight and awareness, repeat statements 1 and 2 in the Reality Check. Were the results different the second time around?

2. Review the story of the two monks, Tanzan and Ekido. Describe, from personal experience, two similar situations where you were unable to let go. Don't worry if what you write is negative. More importantly, make it a valuable learning experience.

Chapter 4

Intention Doing/Being

It is no small thing to compose a sonata or write a perceptive novel; we are indebted to the great composers and writers who have given us beauty and insight into human nature. But I am most moved by the beauty of the perfectly crafted life, where every bit of selfishness has been carved away and what is thought, felt, said and done are brought into harmony.

—Eknath Easwaran, *Meditation: A Simple Eight-Point Program*

We spend most of our life energies in doing. Think of all the effort students expend in learning/doing: taking courses, attending lectures, writing notes, solving problems, completing and handing in essays, studying for exams, writing exams ... the list is endless. Outside of school, we also have a long list of activities. How much free time does one really have every day? Of course, the amount of free time varies from person to person, but generally it is small.

Notwithstanding, the doing is relatively important. But does all this doing pay off in the long term, and is it necessary?

In a study on optimal conditions for college student learning, researchers suggest that the brain works best when:

- It is rested.
- It is hydrated.
- It is unstressed.
- It enjoys itself.

Note the importance here of finding time to relax and unwind in order to achieve an optimal level for learning—take time "to be."

Even the hardworking Donald Trump writes in his book *Trump 101*: "Being successful in business requires much more than hard work and good ideas. You have to be persistent, confident, curious, flexible, passionate, patient, and in love with what you're doing."[1]

We are so immersed in the doing part of life. We are told that if we put in enough doing, we will have a successful career. What a motivator! The rules are simple: just study hard, read a lot, go to school, get good grades, acquire a job, work hard, and become a productive person. All that is required is a personal effort. The personal effort, however, may have negative outcomes: "Heart attacks, ulcers, headaches, alcoholism, drug abuse, broken families, traffic jams, insomnia and poor digestion are all direct results of doing too much," writes Fred Gratzon in his book *The Lazy Way to Success*.[2]

Personal Reflections

Often when I pose the question, "What is a 'being' person?" I receive a blank stare from my students. When I ask the seemingly impossible question, "How can you become a 'being' person?" the facial expressions I observe (because there are no verbal responses) suggest that I must be from another planet to ask such a question. A somewhat easier —trick—question is, "What do you want to be?" A frequent answer I hear is, "I want to be a ... (salesperson, lawyer, accountant, technologist, etc.)" which, of course, is what the responder wants to *do*. The lack of response to these questions points to the fact that students do not know what being really means. Countless hours at school, much money, and enormous effort spent pleasing our teachers and employers means working to the limit of our capacity. What would happen if, after all the toil, you found yourself without a job? One hopes you would cope, but many would be devastated, their self-worth in question. If you can separate who you are from what you do, you will soon realize that your self-worth has not changed one iota. Otherwise, you have not separated the essence of who you are from what you have done. It is so easy—but incorrect—to identify the self with what one has accomplished. A significant change in my life occurred when I decided to change my career completely. Separating my self from my previous work was liberating; in fact, I finally found freedom from an uninspiring job. The change worked wonders for me.

Turning the Self Inside Out

What Does This Have to Do with Me?

We easily lose sight of who we are and become identified with what we do. A TV commercial asks, "What makes you uniquely Canadian?" Some of the responses are, "I play hockey," "I drink Labatt's beer," "I spend most holidays at the lake." These very special doing things show that our idea of being a Canadian is associated with something that we perform, rather than who we are.

Imagine that you are at a party and want to socialize and meet someone new. You ask the person's name, and then your next question is, "So, what do you do?" Small talk, perhaps, but in reality, we talk more easily about what we do than who we are. We put people in a nice little box once we know what they do. We identify, give labels to the person we have just met. This labeling is much easier than really getting to know the actual person.

In a study of rescuers of Jews in World War II, researchers tried to find out if they shared a common link.[3] Those they researched were not Jews, yet they had risked their lives to save Jews who were hunted by the Nazis. The researchers found a common element among the rescuers. They did not think of what they were doing as particularly heroic. They did not really even focus on their acts because they had a sense of who they were. So who were they? People who were simply trying to rescue condemned people. Their sense of being was far greater than their thoughts about doing.

Our present life demands so much of our time. We are inflicted with a "busy sickness." Too many students take on heavy course loads and add even more with part-time work. In order to improve the bottom line, employers demand far too much from their workers. Have we gone too far with doing more? Apparently we have, if we measure the number of work days lost to stress-related problems. The World Health Organization reports that 75 percent of patients in doctors' offices are there because of stress-related problems or illnesses.[4] Does this represent an increase over time? In a study conducted by the U.S. Department of Labor, more than 26 percent of men and 11 percent of women worked fifty hours per week or more in the year 2000. These figures represent an increase of 38 percent over the previous three decades.[5] We have lost much of our freedom to doing.

Our being goes much deeper than what we do. If we simply focus on what we do, our consciousness stays on the external surface. Our doing makes each one of us different, as in the TV commercial. When we focus on who we are, we see the similarities. We are at a much deeper level, like the Nazi rescuers. When we embrace the root of our being and understand who we are; we change our actions. The things we do come from the heart.

In answer to the question, "What uniquely identifies a Canadian?" our discussion above might lead to, "We are peace-loving protectors of nature and our natural resources." Simply stating what we do does not make us Canadian. Rather who we are makes us Canadian. Now do you know what to ask when you meet someone new at the next party?

Turning the Self Inside Out

Reality Check

For each statement below, answer "yes" or "no" under the rating column.

Statement	Rating
1. Do you believe your life is too busy?	_____
2. On a typical day, do you dislike the time spent at work or school?	_____
3. Is making a lot of money a major goal in your career choice?	_____
4. Do you believe that self-reflection is a waste of time?	_____
5. Do you believe that the end result is more important than the means?	_____
Score (add up the "yes" answers, and write the sum)	_____

Interpretation

More "yes" answers (three or more) than "no" means you are a "doing" person. More "no" answers implies you are a "being" person. This book is leading you toward the inner self (a "being" person). If you answered "yes" to more than one of the questions above, and you would like more guidance to your inner self, then read the next section.

Things to Try

1. Wherever you wrote a "yes" answer above, identify ways that would enable you to change your answer to a "no."

2. Where you wrote a "yes" answer above, find someone who recorded a "no" and listen to his/her point of view.

3. For the last statement on the list above, do a SWOT (**S**trength, **W**eaknesses, **O**pportunities, **T**hreats; see http://en.wikipedia.org/wiki/Swot_analysis) analysis on a "yes" answer and another SWOT analysis on a "no" answer.

4. Visit Fred Gratzon's Web site at: http://www.lazyway.net/.

Chapter 5

Reality Beliefs/Truths

Reality is merely an illusion, albeit a very persistent one.

—Albert Einstein

What we achieve inwardly will change our outer reality.

—Otto Rank

Whatever we plant in our subconscious mind and nourish with repetition and emotion will one day become a reality.

—Earl Nightingale

Whatever you believe with feeling becomes your reality.

—Brian Tracy

There is an objective reality out there, but we view it through the spectacles of our beliefs, attitudes, and values.

—David G. Myers

What is reality? The answer may surprise you. An accepted definition of reality is: "The state of things as they actually exist." This definition is dependent on seeing things as they really are. Ask any criminal lawyer about the dependability of witnesses, and the lawyer will admit that witness reliability is quite low. Psychological studies indicate that human beings are very poor at identifying people they saw only once a short time ago, or a few times separated by longer periods of time. The studies reveal error rates are as high as 50 percent[1]—a frightening statistic, given that many convictions are based on the testimony of a witness.

Why, under certain circumstances, can we depend on our memory, and at other times we distort reality completely? There are countless reasons, and here are just a few to consider: perception, objective importance, culture, religion, age, health, stress, past experiences, self-confidence, mood, fatigue, beliefs, biases, prejudices. Consequently, our judgment of what actually takes place is very questionable.

Even more disheartening is our concept of understanding and acceptance of perceived truths. Does our mind comprehend the difference between beliefs, truths, and fiction? Do we know what is really true? Let's look at some earlier discoveries in science. Centuries ago, some people thought that the earth was flat. Most scientists accepted the fact unequivocally. Back in the 1500s, scientists believed that the solar system revolved around the Earth, only to find out in the 1700s that the sun is the center of our solar system. And does the sun rise and set every day? Well, in space, the sun neither rises nor sets. Beliefs create reality and influence our perception of what is. A change in a belief causes a change in our reality. Some things believed to be true centuries ago are now thought to be completely false. What beliefs do we have today that will turn out to be wrong in the future? Where does truth lie? What is your reality? Are you sure that you really know? Scientists were so certain of their convictions in the past that to think otherwise was heresy.

Normally, we function with our thinking mind and trust its interpretation explicitly. At other times, when we experience deeper insights, we discredit the interpretations, since our mind is unable to give a precise label to the experience. We believe that a label is needed in order to understand.

Let us examine this deeper mind further. Imagine a walk through the forest in pursuit of a better understanding of reality. As we enter the forest, we envision the unspoiled beauty of nature. The sights and sounds and feel of the forest capture us—all is clear and real. Everything in the forest exists only in the moment of direct perception in the "being" mind. Existentially, it is as it is, and there is no question of anything else.

As we let go of the rational thinking mind, we find a purer sense of reality. We gain an ability to respond objectively to what is. Does this mean we discount the rational mind? No, we need the rational mind all the time: to learn, to find our way through life, for survival. However, we now know that our thinking, rational mind is fraught with biases, conjectures, beliefs, and illusions. Our rational mind is an excellent tool, a great servant, but a terrible master.

Personal Reflections

There is an exercise I often try in a business class. I start off by stating, "This is all about perception and how we communicate our perception of the world to another person." I proceed to pair off the class, with students in each pair sitting back-to-back. One member in the pair receives a set of instructions that simply identifies an object, such as an ant. The person receiving the instructions then proceeds to help the other person draw the ant on a sheet of paper without naming the object. I give an example to the class: "Take your pencil and move it to the center of your page about one inch from the left, draw a line about half an inch ..." The purpose of the exercise is for one person to attempt to explain his/her perception to the other person. You would be amazed at the interpretations of what is real based on the same set of instructions. Having repeated this exercise many times, I have concluded that what is drawn has little resemblance to the real object. Each one of us has his/her own unique sense of reality. How we describe it varies from person to person. What does this suggest? We are poor communicators and listeners, and what is real to one person is nearly impossible for another person to interpret. We can never know what the other person is feeling, seeing, hearing, smelling, or tasting. This, however, does not change reality; a rose is always a rose and will never be anything else, no matter how we interpret it.

What Does This Have to Do with Me?

We deal best with reality at the depths of our being. Our rational, doing mind is important, but not for seeing things as they are. When we observe, hear, and listen, we need to do so with our full attention. We need to see things as they are, not only as they seem. The tree in the forest must be seen purely, without any filters or prejudgments. We have conflict because I say the tree is the biggest in the forest. You say it is not even close. A debate commences, and a heated exchange of words follows. You say Iran is a peace-loving nation. I say otherwise. The heated exchange becomes words of anger. Why do we let this happen? We formulate our opinions and arguments from the rational mind, which in many ways is irrational. How would our inner being respond to the assertion about Iran? From the inner depths of our being, we know that, "The actions in some countries are a manifestation of past events and inflamed by today's perception. And whatever seed we plant today will become a reality tomorrow." This statement is a truism that could be the foundation for a better future.

Can we see things as they really are all the time? Probably not. In the drama of life, we need both our thinking mind and our "being" mind. Thinking and being play off against each other. We have some conflict within us. But if only the thinking mind took a lesser role, and our being a greater role, our perception of reality would be based on seeing things as they are and not as they seem (conjectures).

We are unaware of most of our thoughts. Our mind, for most of the day, is out of control. How can we gain control of our thoughts? All we need to do is observe with complete attention. Do we observe the tree with full attention? Full attention means not labeling the tree—no internal dialogue, no filters—simply seeing the tree in quietness. The observing becomes the understanding. You cannot observe with full attention through the thinking mind, but you certainly can do this through the wisdom of the inner self.

Reality Check

Reflect on whether you agree or disagree with each of the following statements. Explain your choice.

Statement

1. You should be aware that there are many definitions of reality. One such definition is: "Reality is simply a decision, and different for every human being."

2. If we do not know where truth lies, "Is our life an illusion?"

3. Bertrand Russell once said, "It has been said that man is a rational animal. All my life I have been searching for evidence which could support this."[2]

4. If reality is based on what is, can there be any shades of gray?

Interpretation

These questions are posed to invoke more thought on the topic of reality. There are no right answers to these questions. Now that you have finished answering or pondering each one, however, ask yourself, "From which mind-set did I answer these questions? Was it traditional, universal, or both?"

Things to Try

1. Read Krishnamurti's interpretation of truth at: http://www.escapefromwatchtower.com/krishnamurti.html.

2. Watch the *What is Truth Video* at: http://www.allaboutphilosophy.org/what-is-truth-video.htm.

3. For general interest, read the article on "Ten Politically Incorrect Truths about Human Nature" from Psychology Today at: http://www.docstoc.com/docs/20232/Psychology-Today_-Ten-Politically-Incorrect-Truths-About-Human-Nature.

Chapter 6

Effort
Struggle/Effortless

Yesterday I watched a boat make its way out to sea. It was a long, heavy boat with four men rowing hard. A battle of man against the forces of Nature, the tide pushing the boat back toward the land, and the oarsmen countering with all their might to move the boat forward. It was a struggle, but eventually the boat moved into the channel and toward the open sea. There was little chance now that the tide would push the boat back to the land. When the battle was won, the four men unfurled the sails, and immediately the sails billowed from the onrushing wind. Now the struggle was over; with the sails fully open, the boat moved effortlessly through the water toward an island on the horizon. If only we could find our sails, and, with the wind behind our backs, move effortlessly through life.

Mihaly Csikszentmihalyi, author of *Flow: The Psychology of Optimal Experience,* describes effortless effort as: "Being completely involved in an activity for its own sake. The ego falls away. Time flies. Every action, movement, and thought follows inevitably from the previous one, like playing jazz. Your whole Being is involved, and you're using your skills to the utmost."[1]

When we hear "effortless," we have the desire to attain this state of being: no struggle, gentle movement, no conflict, easily acquired. If, however, we are to make it our goal to achieve, we are engaged in yet another struggle—to gain that which we do not have. This is the paradox: by trying (making it a goal), we again put on the wheels of struggle, and the goal may ultimately get away from us. It does sound strange to the old mind-set: "By not doing, we have more chance of reaching our goal." Once the sails of the boat are fully deployed, has not the struggle to move the boat ceased? No more effort is needed. Our mind needs to be in the same state in order to remove the struggle.

Analogy aside, how do we accomplish this? We need to shift to the new paradigm by "being involved for its own sake," as Csikszentmihalyi suggests. Initially, it requires some effort: concentration, focus, awareness. But with time, being takes precedence. Once the focus of attention is removed from the periphery of struggle and moves to a single point of reference (full attention to the task), then the mind shifts from the object of the struggle to an understanding of struggle. As with an accomplished jazz musician, each action naturally flows into the next action gently, with ease, without struggle.

Even more is behind this shift of mind-set. If we allow our old mind-set to continue, the internal dialogue predetermines to what extent the task is easy or hard. The old mind-set says, "I don't feel like studying for the upcoming exam." This type of comment creates negativity toward the task at hand and adds to the struggle. Just imagine for a moment that the oarsmen in the boat decided it was impossible to move the boat against the wind. They would struggle not only against the elements, but also within themselves. By focusing only on the task for "its own sake," we put all our effort into the task, remove the struggle within, and feel a sense of effortless effort.

When I asked the oarsmen in the boat whether it was an effort, they responded with great pride that it was effortless effort because, "We were all completely involved and knew we would succeed."

Personal Reflections

Many of my students worry about how they will complete an assignment in the allotted time. "So many tests and assignments to do. I will never finish on time," they argue. Likewise, I hear from graduates of the program about how busy they are with their new job. "The demands of the job are unreasonable," they suggest. I do empathize with their situation, but the bottom line is that the assignment must be completed; procrastinating and complaining only add to the frustration. Young people have so many diverse interests that completing an assignment is hard work and often not enjoyable. The first prerequisite, I tell them, is to dismiss any intruding thoughts and remove any unrelated activities. Not so easy when you are told what to do and someone invites you over for a pizza, or surfing the Internet for a vacation spot sounds more exciting. The second prerequisite is to give the task your full attention. In one of his movies, Jackie Chan asks his protégé to spend the afternoon washing and waxing his car each day for a week. "Find joy in every task that you undertake; otherwise life will be a struggle," Jackie asserts. Attend to the job at hand, and give it your full attention. Whenever a task seems distasteful to me, I have found that the more attention I give to the task, the more satisfying it becomes. We tend to think that unpleasantness is a quality of the job; more often it is a condition of the mind.

What Does This Have to Do with Me?

Apparently, our perception largely determines the extent of the effort required. Schoolwork for some is an arduous task: fear of failure, writing exams, time constraints all label the task as a struggle. At work we also give to the task labels that become further hindrances: "It's boring." "Is it necessary?" Others find school and work to be a joy, easy to do, effortless because they are focused on the task. They even accept failure with a positive attitude: a former student of mine was happy when he failed an exam. When I asked how he could be pleased with a failing grade, he said, "I usually do very well on all my exams, and for the first time I didn't. I have found something I don't understand and with it an opportunity to learn. I know with a little more effort I will be successful the next time." How could you possibly enjoy failure? This student's perception was that failure guaranteed future success.

The second requisite, mentioned above, is to give the task your full attention. This requisite is much easier to fulfill if you are able to discover those things that you really enjoy. Select a career that will bring you satisfaction and joy. The real reward is that all tasks immediately become acts of effortlessness effort.

Reality Check

For each statement below, answer "yes" or "no" under the rating column.

Statement	Rating
1. Based on this chapter, do you think washing the dishes could be a joyful task?	_____
2. Do you believe that struggling may be related to having an inferiority complex?	_____
3. "Struggle is a conflict between *what we are* and *what we want to be*." Do you agree?	_____
4. Has this chapter given you some insight into why we struggle? Has your perception changed in any way?	_____
Score (add up the "yes" answers, and write the sum)	**_____**

Interpretation

For each of the questions above, answering "yes" would be better, based on the chapter presentation. Don't be overly concerned if you answered "no" to any of these questions.

Things to Try

1. Look at the Web site that references Mihaly Csikszentmihalyi's article, *All about Flow*: <http://www.37signals.com/svn/posts/104-all-about-flow>.

2. Check out two books by J. Krishnamurti, which should be in your public library; they are particularly informative on the chapter topic: *Commentaries on Living: Series Two* (San Francisco: Quest Books, 1967) and *Think on These Things* (New York: Harper Perennial, 1989).

3. Read the chapter titled "Wholehearted Efforts Bring Real Results," pp.166–174, in Dr. Henry Cloud's new book, *The Secret Things of God*.

Chapter 7

Learning Resistance/Acceptance

We cannot teach people anything; we can only help them discover it within themselves.

—Galileo

An often-used saying is, "We can lead a horse to water but never make the horse drink." In terms of education, we could rephrase this saying and write, "We can provide the environment and opportunity for students to learn, but unless they have the thirst, the students will resist, and the learning will be inconsequential." Perhaps the most important task for the teacher is to effect the learning, to modify the behavior so that the student develops an appetite to learn. Equally, the student has a responsibility. The student, through self-discovery, ensures that the learning is significant.

Educators do not simply need knowledge about their subject matter; they also need knowledge of each student and his/her needs. When teachers act as mentors and facilitators, they influence learning positively. If teaching is to be effective and have any significant impact on the student, there should be a harmonious blend between teaching a subject and teaching a student.

In the circle of learning, good teaching will help someone learn, but ultimately the learner has to be responsible for his/her learning. There is much written on the topic from a learner's perspective. All students, however, can improve their ability to learn. We will look primarily at the learner's attitude and behavior.

First, we must accept the educational system as it exists and then look for ways to maximize our learning. Many students at college expend enormous amounts of negative energy complaining about their classmates and instructors, avoiding their homework, and adding barriers to their learning. As an example, consider what happens when we read a book that is of little interest to us. We have to put aside other things, which are probably far more appealing. We procrastinate, become annoyed, stress out—all negative emotional responses. Eventually, through effort and concentration, we recognize and complete the task—accept what is. Once we accept what has to be done, our mind relaxes, positive energy replaces negative feelings, and learning becomes a new adventure. Over time, we may even find joy in what we are doing. Our new mind-set suggests that learning requires much less effort than we originally believed, and we are able to complete the task successfully. We can extend this further into everything we do—not only tasks related to school, but tasks in other life situations.

In summary, caring teachers who affectively connect with their students, and learners who have a positive attitude toward learning, can create a bridge that links an enthusiastic learner with the joy of learning.

Personal Reflections

One of the primary goals of education is to modify a student's behavior so that learning becomes a positive experience. A student, however, cannot be simply willed to accept the teaching and possibly change his/her attitude toward learning. Each term, I start a new semester with a course outline. In broad terms, I inform my class what will be covered and state my expectations of the class and of each student. I notice that some of my students react emotionally—they appear shocked and go into avoidance mode. These students seem to be thinking, "You can't be serious, there is no way I am going to ..." or, "Let me out of this class. I want to talk to the department head." If this student continues with the course, I often notice that they test my resolve and often complain to me, "I have five quizzes, four papers, three presentations, two meetings, and a partridge to take care of next week. How can you expect my project at the same time?" Be assured, most instructors have heard it all. The next stage I notice is eventual surrender and acceptance. "This teacher is not yielding to my complaints. I guess I'd better do it." If they stick with it, amazing things will happen. Initially, the student struggles, but then s/he gains confidence and experiences success and a good feeling. Often the student admits, "It wasn't bad, after all. Why did I resist in the first place?" Self-discovery takes place. Indeed a positive outcome. Of course, educators can help students overcome a negative attitude toward the course, but how much more effective would it be if the student became aware of the stages of his/her own resistance, accepted responsibility for the workload, and got down to being productive?

What Does This Have to Do with Me?

This chapter identifies two key elements of an educational process and describes how they affect the student in a traditional school. The first deals with pedagogy (the delivery of knowledge), and the second one focuses on the learner (the recipient of knowledge).

Caring instructors who can affectively implement the curriculum and students who have a positive attitude toward the learning environment are the hallmark of effective learning. As a student, you can do much to enhance the learning environment. Accept the conditions, but be cognizant of what is lacking. Work to your full potential. Try the new mind-set approach mentioned above. Enjoy the adventure of learning. This approach will add much, not only to your schooling, but to your life skills.

Based on the discussion in this chapter, we now know the importance of acceptance and an open mind. If we give our full attention to learning, the learner and learning blend harmoniously into a unified whole—the learner and the learning become one and the same. We also know what happens if we resist—we separate the learner from the content of learning. We assume, too, that if our learning is significant (i.e., the learning is not just fact-based but is integrated and affects the overall well-being and behavior of the learner), it will complement the learner's needs.

Reality Check

For each statement below, answer "yes" or "no" under the rating column.

Statement	Rating
1. The message of this chapter is to accept everything blindly.	_____
2. Can you explain the difference between the effective and affective domain in teaching? If not, do some research on the Web.	_____
3. One thesis in this chapter is that education is distinctly different from life issues.	_____
4. Do you believe that merely acquiring knowledge constitutes an education?	_____
Score (add up the "no" answers, and write the sum)	_____

Interpretation

For each of the questions above, you probably answered "no," based on the chapter presentation. Do you need more reference material? If so, go to Things to Try.

Things to Try

A number of concepts mentioned in this chapter were taken from the field of holistic education, which is based on the premise that the learner finds identity, meaning, and purpose through connections internally and externally.

1. There are some wonderful articles on holistic education. One that will serve as an introduction is: http://www.holistic-education.net/visitors.htm.

2. Also: http://www.putnampit.com/holistic.html will provide further insight.

3. Research the David Lynch Foundation at: http://www.davidlynchfoundation.org/.

4. More complete literature is available from authors such as Scott H. Forbes, John P. Miller, and Parker Palmer.

5. For a philosophical approach to education, read J. Krishnamurti's *The Awakening of Intelligence*.

Chapter 8

Control
Mind Problems/Mind Control

Imagine driving a car and not being in control. The car would route itself and end up taking us wherever. If our destination was a movie with a special friend and the car (uncontrollably) ended up taking us on sightseeing venture, we would have a serious problem. What a dilemma. If this were your car, you would lose out on an enjoyable experience and would undoubtedly irritate your friend.

Would we deliberately allow this to happen to us? Of course not. But wait. Most of us allow our mind to take us on a ride. Are we in control of the thoughts that pass through our mind? Consciously, we are doing what we want to do in life; unconsciously, however, we have very little control. In St. Augustine's words: "I can tell my hand what to do and it will do it instantly. Why won't my mind do what I say?"[1]

Few people enjoy the company of individuals who talk incessantly. Yet many of us tolerate the chatter that originates within our own minds. Just for a moment, listen to the chatter that resonates through the mind from the perspective of a detached observer. Only when we become increasingly aware of our patterns of thought, do we gradually learn to control the character of our mind.

Not only do we have little control within ourselves, but through social engineering our mind is trained to believe whatever is the propaganda of the day. We are bombarded with media and mass programming—the Internet, computer games and social networking, television, movies, music, newspapers, magazines, books. These are commonplace in our everyday lives. Through the media and communication networks, an entire community can be controlled with relative ease. The question arises, have we surrendered our freedom to advances in technology? The danger of our loss of freedom is expressed in the following fable: "A man found an eagle's egg and put it in the nest of a barnyard hen. The eaglet hatched with the brood of chicks and grew up with them. All his life, the eagle did what the barnyard chicks did, thinking he was a barnyard chicken. Years passed, and the eagle grew old. One day he saw a magnificent bird above him in the cloudless sky. The old eagle looked up in awe. 'Who's that?' he asked. 'That's the eagle, the king of the birds,' said his neighbor. 'He belongs to the sky. We belong to the Earth; we're chickens.' So the eagle lived and died as a chicken, for that's what he was told he was."[2]

We may not want to be controlled and manipulated, but it seems that outside influences and uncontrollable thoughts render us slaves to our mind. We can liberate our mind through a process of conscious awareness. People with conscious awareness can tell their mind what to do. Think success, think happiness, and your destiny will be those thoughts; and you will cease to be an eagle who thought he was a chicken.

Personal Reflections

When you control your mind, you are no longer at its mercy; you have found liberation from a mind that, for most, is out of control. Instead of thoughts controlling you, your new mind has control of your thoughts. This is a win situation on all accounts. You will find through mindfulness that you will become a more effective worker, be more aware of your behavior, have improved relationships, enjoy better health, feel more energy, improve your interpersonal and communication skills, and feel psychologically fit: well-adjusted and happier with life. All this improvement begs the question: "Why are most people not aware of their thoughts and why do they not enjoy the freedom that comes with mindfulness?" When you see moment by moment what is occurring, you don't get lost in thinking. As we begin developing this choiceless awareness, what happens is quite amazing. I have noted the benefits at various levels: at retreats, with youth groups, in crisis situations, with addictions. Based on the testimonials I have received, it has always been a positive experience accompanied by lifelong benefits.

Turning the Self Inside Out

What Does This Have to Do with Me?

A wonderful book, just recently published, talks about the mind and how to take control of your thoughts. Perhaps you have read it: *The Secret*, by Rhonda Byrne. The book discusses the possibility of attaining a power equivalent to tapping into all the resources available in the universe. "You create your life through your thoughts.... When you become aware of your thoughts, then you become aware of how incredibly powerful you are."[3]

To control the mind and realize its unlimited power has the potential to unleash the genie in the bottle who does all at your command. The only thing you need to do is make a slight change to your mind-set. Anyone can do this. The change starts within, the part of you over which you have complete control. You do not have control over events and circumstances, but you do have control over how you interpret them.

Through mindfulness, you can choose whatever you want to think about. You simply need to replace habitual nonproductive thinking with complete awareness and thoughtful attention. Back to the car scenario. Are you not in control when you park your car at the shopping mall? You make a mental note of the location so that when you return, you can find your car. Similarly, you practice mindfulness when driving, and your car responds to your commands. The same situation occurs with the mind. If you wish to make a U-turn, your mind will respond accordingly, as long as you are in control. When your mind responds to your wishes, you have mastered the art of living. We will learn specific techniques about mindfulness as we progress through this book.

Reality Check

For each statement below, answer "yes" or "no" under the rating column.

Statement	Rating
1. Do you agree that you have little control of the thoughts that enter your mind?	_____
2. Do you understand the concept of social engineering? If not, do an Internet search.	_____
3. Do you agree with the statement that, without mindfulness, you encourage mind problems?	_____
4. Do you believe that you are what you think?	_____
Score (add up the "yes" answers, and write the sum)	**_____**

Interpretation

For each of the questions above, you should have answered "yes," based on the chapter presentation. For any "no," consider why a "yes" answer would be appropriate.

Things to Try

1. An easy read and well worth the effort is the book by Rhonda Byrne titled *The Secret*.

2. Related to the topic "how to control thoughts," add any comments or experiences to our blog at: http://turningselfinsideout.blogspot.com/ as a Chapter 8 posting.

Chapter 9

Time
Time Bound/Timelessness

Thought is time. Thought is born of experience and knowledge, which are inseparable from time and the past. Time is the psychological enemy of man. Our action is based on knowledge and therefore time, so man is always a slave to the past. Thought is ever-limited and so we live in constant conflict and struggle. There is no psychological evolution.

—J. Krishnamurti, *The Ending of Time*

How can time be an enemy? Of course, Krishnamurti is not referring to the usual concept of clock time, as in the time to get from point A to point B. We all realize the importance of clock time, the necessity to "do" something over a period of hours, days, weeks. There is another dimension of time, however, which, in contrast to clock time, is called psychological time. This psychological time is the timeless dimension of being in which there is no beginning or end. Let us elaborate further.

One important purpose of your training at college is to secure satisfactory employment after graduation. Once you have found a job, additional time will be required to become successful—probably many years. Does this success guarantee psychological well-being? With success, will we find fulfillment, happiness? Many people are successful in their job but generally unhappy with life. Success takes time; happiness is timeless. Unfortunately, we mistake doing, in the dimension of time, as the ultimate path toward our happiness. Jim Collins, author of Good to Great, said of the fourteen greatest CEOs in American corporate history—those who stood out as exceptional business leaders—that about half trashed their personal lives in the process.[1]

To become a CEO or VP of a company is no easy task. A lot of "doing" time is required. Once achieved, though, the CEO or VP position in the corporation is tenuous, and at the end of the day, the executive leaves and relinquishes the position. A lot of time spent on "doing," only to lose it all.

Here is an example to consider. If your purpose at college is to get good grades this semester, then time will be required, beneficial only until you start the following semester, when you have to do it all again. Not unlike the CEO who experiences temporary professional success. However, college can be much more than this. College is an opportunity to attain personal success. Personal success is about effective communication, respecting others, a caring attitude, a positive role model, dedication and commitment, accepting responsibility, self-confidence, strong values and ethics. Personal success is permanent, life-enduring, timeless.

Time is always either in the past or future; timelessness is in the present moment. Good grades are goals in the future and therefore time-bound. Being respectful of others, displaying a caring attitude, accepting responsibility, and helping a classmate are moment by moment occurrences. In this mode, time is not important: whatever we are doing in the very moment is the focus of our attention. Doing becomes integrated with this timeless mode, which is the earmark of personal success.

Think of applying presence to a job situation—for example, a salesperson in a retail store. Selling the article is important—a goal that will take time, but we know personal success is when we surrender to the timeless moment. Just imagine how the customers would feel if they received our full attention.

Personal Reflections

After high school graduation, a dear friend of mine began his working career with a paint company. He worked hard and successfully climbed the corporate ladder, and, after many years, eventually became vice president. He commanded a six-figure salary, traveled a lot, presented at international conferences, and was renowned and respected in the industry. During a recent high school reunion, I had the opportunity to spend an evening with my dear friend. I congratulated him and told him how proud I felt knowing him. To my surprise, he then proceeded to tell me how unhappy he was. In his position of vice president, he continues to work twelve-hour days and some weekends. I asked, "Why not give it up? You have certainly accomplished everything you desire—success, respect, money." "It is not that easy," he told me. "I now have the status in the community, the salary to support the high standard of living my family enjoys, a position in the company that I have worked so hard to attain, and I am not willing to surrender. But yet I am miserable. I hate the long hours, the traveling, the decisions, and the responsibilities. Even relationships with my family are questionable. I find I have no time for myself; other people and situations take every minute away from me. I am left with nothing."

What Does This Have to Do with Me?

Timelessness is a difficult concept for some. Many people relate only to clock time and never give psychological time any thought. Timelessness, though, is a natural perspective. Very young children have little understanding of the passing of time. As we become more aware, we find ourselves less addicted to clock time.

If you are still unsure of the difference, the following may help: try to explain to a four-year-old the concept of clock time, about the next hour or tomorrow. For a four-year-old, time is now. Asking a four-year-old to go and fetch something from the upstairs bedroom may mean a climb up a mountain of stairs, a slide down the stairs on a cushion, and a return with the fetched object fifteen minutes later, or even a return without the item. Our grown-up understanding of time is fundamentally different. For the child, life is the timelessness moment. For the adult, life is measured by clock time. Eventually, we teach the child about the logistics of life, the importance of every minute, and the four-year-old forgets how to dawdle in the snow, talk to the alley cat, or make a wish upon a star.

As you look toward your future years at school and eventually attaining a rewarding career, you will need to plan for a happy future. In your plan, you will need to balance personal happiness with professional success, based on what you have read in this chapter. Do not discount either one. Like the four-year-old, try to find moments when time is not important, and joyful presence is your primary goal.

Reality Check

For each statement below, give a rating from 1 to 5. 1 no, 2 slightly, 3 somewhat, 4 more than not, 5 yes.

Statement	Rating
1. Do you have a firm understanding of the difference between clock time and psychological time?	_____
2. Based on the concepts presented in this chapter, would you say that schools should focus on the complete person (holistic education) and not just grades (success)?	_____
3. Based on the concepts presented in this chapter, should employers put more emphasis on values and ethics, and less on production?	_____
4. Do you agree with the statement that living moment by moment is a guarantee of achieving a successful life?	_____
5. Do you agree with the statement that, "If you succeed in your professional life yet are unsuccessful in your personal life, ultimately you have failed?"	_____
Score (Add up the numbers in the rating column, and write the sum)	_____

Interpretation

The maximum possible is 25. The higher the number (the closer to 25), the more your mind-set is tending toward the timeless dimension.

Things to Try

1. Try out the moment by moment concept explained in the chapter for part of a day, and experience the changes that take place.

2. What can you do to become less time-conscious and live on a moment by moment basis? Identify at least three things you can do, and post them on our blogspot at http://turningselfinsideout.blogspot.com under Chapter 9.

3. Write a definition for "professional success" and "personal success." Then identify how you can attain both these types of success.

4. Visit Jim Collins's Web site at: http://www.jimcollins.com/.

Chapter 10

Health
Negative/Positive Thinking

> *The question frequently asked is, "When a person has manifested a disease in the body or some kind of discomfort in their life, can it be turned around through the power of right thinking?" The answer is absolutely, yes.*
>
> —Rhonda Byrne, *The Secret*

Many medical doctors and their patients, particularly in our western civilization, are concerned that we are overmedicated. The fear is that, over the long-term, medication might have a negative effect on our physical well-being, even cause other symptoms and further complications. In many cases, such as high blood pressure, the medicine controls but does not cure the problem. Medicines might succeed in hiding the pain, inhibiting the illness, even prolonging life, but has the medical profession eradicated the disease or even identified the root cause? "Indeed, physicians and doctors of all schools should learn the causes of disease and complications, and they should all learn to realize that to mask symptoms with their drugs and treatments is to stand in their own light."[1]

Strong evidence now supports the statement from *The Secret* that opens this chapter. A useful approach would be to look carefully at the person and not treat the effect of an ailment. Each one of us has the potential to cure common illnesses that regularly afflict us. Many stories, even from people we know, indicate that they focus their attention on their ailment, and, like a self-fulfilling prophesy, what they think is what they receive. If we think negatively about an ailment—for example, "This headache is terrible"—then the headache may continue and possibly intensify. Changing the thought pattern and responding either by accepting the situation (no thoughts) or encouraging positive thoughts (such as, "This headache is just temporary. It will go away") will do much to alleviate the symptom. Letting go of negative thoughts will give the body a chance to heal itself.

Our physical bodies are self-generating organisms. Deepak Chopra, in his audiotape *Perfect Health*, claims that our body replenishes itself with new cells: the eyes in two days, the intestinal lining in five to thirty days, the liver in six weeks, the bones in five months.[2] Dr. Chopra points to the fact that our body is a natural pharmacy. In fact, most prescribed medicines are self-generated within our body. We have enormous potential to heal ourselves. Through a holistic approach and the power of positive thinking, we can rid our body of many ailments and diseases.

A report from the Mayo Clinic[3] indicates that through the power of positive thinking we can expect:

- Decreased negative stress
- Greater resistance to catching the common cold

- A sense of well-being and improved health
- Reduced risk of coronary artery disease
- Easier breathing if we have certain lung diseases, such as emphysema
- Improved coping ability for women with high-risk pregnancies
- Better coping skills during hardships

How easy is it to change negative thoughts into positive ones? James J. Asher, in his book *Brainswitching: A Skill for the 21st Century*, suggests a technique that works for easing pain and many other ailments. Brainswitching is an attempt to "jam" the focus on negative feelings until the brain shifts out of an anxious mode to a more neutral mode. The technique involves choosing a neutral thought in advance, and using it whenever we have a negative thought or feeling. The thought could be a mantra, or even a silly phrase such as "Green fried tomatoes." Initially, a little effort is needed to concentrate on your neutral or nonsense thought. By your continually interrupting negative thoughts, the pain will eventually lessen.

Personal Reflections

Healthy living is teamwork. It should be the concern not only of the individual, but also of the family and the community. In early years, good health habits are the responsibility of the family. In adulthood, we understand the importance of a doctor, and we seek support from the community and our significant other. To a large extent, concern with my well-being is shared by my wife, and, to a lesser extent, by my doctor. It is important that health be a concerted, combined effort. When you choose a life partner, that person can have a major influence on your health. My wife ensures that I: eat the proper foods, exercise appropriately, curb any excessive habits, am aware of my sleeping patterns, relax when stressed, spend time with friends, protect my skin when sunbathing, even maintain a high-functioning capacity (encouraging me to write this book). It is important that you have a life partner who takes an interest in your well-being. My annual doctor's visit is important. The doctor validates my health habits and recognizes the important role we play in keeping physically, emotionally, and socially fit. We are who we work at being.

What Does This Have to Do with Me?

Adopt a sensible health pattern when you're young. The best time to do this is right now. Don't wait for tomorrow. Here is sound advice from Pulitzer Prize–winner Dr. Robert N. Butler, professor of geriatrics at Mount Sinai School of Medicine and president of the International Longevity Center:

- Eat less; put your fork down after every mouthful and eat more slowly.
- Boost your consumption of fruits and vegetables; eat slowly and enjoy the taste.
- Consume less fat; bring awareness while eating.
- Quit smoking and drink moderately; think about the potential damage of smoking and drinking excessively.
- Take a baby aspirin (81 mg) every day.
- Walk or jog in the sun, with suitable sunscreen protection, for thirty minutes every day; be observant of nature.
- Get more sleep.
- Relax; meditate at different times during the day.
- Try to connect with happy people (see next chapter).
- Find a purpose and enjoy a better quality of life.
- Exercise your brain; try crossword and math puzzles, board games, cards.

Also, learn to turn negative thinking into positive thinking. Admittedly, it takes practice—you are creating a new habit, after all. If you are feeling ill or you are seized by a bad feeling, stop and evaluate what you're thinking. If you find that your thoughts are negative, try "brainswitching." When you feel that you are sliding into a state of negative thinking, internally repeat your chosen word/phrase. Keep up the monologue until you feel better. You'll soon get the hang of it.

Reality Check

For each statement below, provide a "yes" or "no" answer. Add up the total of "yes" answers, and write the sum in the score row below.

Statement	Rating
1. Do you believe that the mind/body has the power to heal?	_____
2. Do you plan to try "brainswitching" in the near future?	_____
3. Have you heard about holistic medicine? If not, research it.	_____
4. Are you careful about taking drugs and prescription medicine?	_____
Score (add up the "yes" answers, and write the sum)	_____

Interpretation

We are looking for "yes" answers in response to the statements above. If you want to investigate this topic further, try the next section.

Things to Try

1. Read Daniel Redwood's interview with Deepak Chopra at: http://www.healthy.net/scr/interview.asp?Id=167.

2. Research some of the Web sites cited in the endnotes to this chapter.

3. Do you have any further suggestions or ideas? Contribute to the blog at: http://turningselfinsideout.blogspot.com/ as a posting for Chapter 10.

Chapter 11

Relationships Share Conditionally/ Give Unconditionally

Some of the biggest challenges in relationships come from the fact that most people enter a relationship in order to get something: They're trying to find someone who's going to make them feel good. In reality, the only way a relationship will last is if you see your relationship as a place that you go to give, and not a place that you go to take.

—Anthony Robbins

Our lives, for the most part, are based on relationships—interpersonal interactions. Relationships are paramount to our psychological well-being. We find much joy in a strong relationship. A strong relationship means that shared experience and communication occur not only in action or in some project work or ideology, but internally, facilitating growth, enhancement, openness, and development.

There is therefore an outer movement, where we do things together, and an inner movement of being and growing together.

The root of a strong relationship is a selfless attitude where we give our self completely. The Golden Rule from the Bible (Luke 6:31) says, treat others the same way you want them to treat you. A simple technique that we can try is to review our actions and our dialogue with other people, and note how they reacted. If the reaction was unfavorable, we can reverse the role and ask how we would respond if we received such a message. This technique is also useful when we have discussions about people who are not privy to our conversation. Pretend the person we discuss is present and listening to the conversation. Would we now be more careful in what we say? Wouldn't everyone want to be treated fairly at all times? Using the technique of reflection and openness would significantly improve work relationships, school relationships, family relationships, all friendships.

Why do we have problems with relationships? What is the root cause? Most relationship problems are caused by the ego. In particular, egos built on the pursuit of self-importance and self-interest. We see this daily with individuals who assert that they are always right and the other person wrong—people who have an insatiable desire for knowledge, success, and wealth in order to establish their superiority. Society may accept some of these (normal) attributes; these ego types, however, do not usually have strong relationships or endearing communication skills. Moreover, they tend to be unhappy.

How, then, can we foster stronger relationships? The ego affects all relationships. Instead of seeking to take from a relationship, we can build a better relationship based on trust, open communication, and mutual respect, and eventually we will break down the walls that were created by the ego. An example might explain. Do you have a pet at home? If you love your animal, you will give unconditionally.

Your self-interest is not at stake, and the animal requires nothing in return. A relationship like this is bound to last forever—it is a place that you go to give, and not a place that you go to take.

Personal Reflections

I have found that connecting immediately with my students on a personal level is invaluable, breaking down the traditional barriers that exist between teacher and students. Each semester when I start a new term, I force myself to learn the names of all my students as quickly as possible. I have an exercise that I practice in order to learn their names on the first day of class. The exercise is called Road to Jerusalem. Here is how we apply the technique in a class situation. Each student in my class has to introduce the students who were introduced up till that point. The exercise is played as follows: The first person states their name and some information about who they are; the second person then states their name, tells a little about who they are, and introduces the first person who came before them; the third person continues with their name and introduces the two people who came before them. We continue the game until the last person, the teacher, has to introduce all those who came before—quite a mental effort, but extremely beneficial. The technique sets a nice precedent for a strong relationship with my students. At all times, I try to remember the Golden Rule: treat my students as I would want to be treated.

What Does This Have to Do with Me?

What is your present situation? Are you at school? Do you have a job? Are you involved in a relationship, perhaps married or have a special commitment? Would you say that you are in love? Does your school or job interfere with your relationship? In today's society, a lot of couples find time management difficult, and they are often unable to connect. Not only is time a problem, but also trying to handle the stress of a career creates problems with a relationship. We live in a world where ambition, success, greed, and desire are acceptable. We follow a self-centered activity, and yet we need psychological security. We depend on our special friend for comfort, pleasure, companionship, attention, love. Our outer ego and our inner psychological needs have to be attended to continuously.

When a problem surfaces with a relationship, look at the root cause. Whatever the effect might be, the root of the problem is often ego-based. Even if your partner complains that you spend too little time together, is this not an issue of the ego wanting more (time)? Remember, from the discussion above, your responsibility is to be aware and recognize the demands of the ego. The communication would certainly break down if you gave a response like, "What am I to do? My job requires that I spend eighty hours a week at work." This is a wrong (defensive) answer. If you recognize that the ego is the root cause, an appropriate (helpful) answer based on giving would be much more effective. A better answer would be, "I am working eighty hours a week on average, and, although it appears that the job requires it, I realize that I need to give you more of my time. Let us work out how we can spend more time together."

Reality Check

For each statement below (for the second question, record the total points), give a rating from 1 to 5. 1 poor, 2 needs improvement, 3 satisfactory, 4 quite good, 5 high. Add up the numbers in the rating column, and write the sum in the score row.

Statement	Rating
1. How would you rate your relationship with your favorite person?	_____
2. For the person above, create a checklist that reads: "What I give to our relationship." Score a quarter point for each (mutually beneficial) statement.	_____
3. Trust, mutual respect, open communication are the cornerstones of all relationships. How would you rate these elements in your special relationship?	_____
4. How well do you communicate your feelings? Do you display openness toward others?	_____
5. How would you rate the quality of the time that you spend with your special friend?	_____
Score (Add up the numbers in the rating column, and write the sum)	_____

Interpretation

Any mark of 18 or more implies that you form strong relationships. But don't despair; scoring less than 18 only indicates that you need to work a little harder. Do you want to improve your relationships?

Do the "Things to Try" below, and remember, this is an exercise in "open communication."

Things to Try

1. Give the above list to your favorite person, and let him/her rank *you* on the same questions.

2. Ask your favorite friend to answer the same questions above and ask if s/he would be willing to share his/her responses.

3. Identify someone whom you believe has strong interpersonal skills. Try to rank the person based on statements 3, 4, and 5 in the Reality Check above. If the person ranks higher than you did, reread the chapter and try to identify where his/her strengths lie.

Chapter 12

Self-Actualization Limited/Complete Awareness of Oneself

If you plan on being anything less than you are capable of being, you will probably be unhappy all the days of your life.

—Abraham Maslow

First, let us gain an initial understanding of self-actualization. The following is taken from the work of Abraham Maslow: "Self-actualization is the desire for self-fulfillment, namely the tendency for the individual to become ... more and more what one is, to become everything that one is capable of becoming."[1]

Maslow coined his hierarchy of needs in the context of humanistic psychology. According to Maslow, four distinct psychological needs must be met before we reach a final stage of self-actualization. This hierarchy ranks needs from lower (basic) to higher (growth):

physiological needs, safety, belongingness, esteem, and finally self-actualization.

Conscious awareness is a requirement for self-actualization: we need to find out who we are, and only then can we "become what we are capable of becoming."

Maslow proposed two different kinds of self-actualizers, the archetypal one, named in his initial work; and a second one, which he identified much later, called the transcendent self-actualizer. Transcendent self-actualizers focus on spiritual aspects: cosmic awareness, unitive consciousness. Transcendents are motivated by beauty, truth, and timelessness.

Maslow's lower four needs are easy to understand and are the basis for a healthy life. We must fulfill our basic needs first: food, water, bodily comforts (physiological); then our safety needs such as security and protection from harm; followed next by: acceptance, love, affiliation with others (belongingness); and esteem, which includes confidence and respect. Maslow's last need, self-actualization, is not as easy to understand and requires further explanation. In my discussion, I will assume that conscious awareness is a prerequisite for self-actualization. This seems to be a fair approach—that we must discover who we are before we are able to reach our full potential.

To discover who we are requires an awareness and understanding of the self. This introspection can be observed when we are involved in doing—experiencing something. Every (human) experience involves three elements, not necessarily in the following order: a sense perception, followed by initial and subsequent thoughts about the experience, and emotional responses to the experience. These three elements are objects of the experience (the effect of the experience), and are separate from the subject of the experience (the person who experiences—i.e., the experiencer). Think of it as follows: When you see something, such as a beautiful sunset, an initial sensation takes place, perhaps goose bumps on your skin; then a response takes place, such as an internally generated thought, like, "Wow, what a wonderful sight," followed by an emotion, say, a desire to hold on to such a beautiful moment. All these are effects of the experience and are observed by the unique you, the experiencer. Separating the experiencer from the experience means that we can view all experiences from within the self. We can observe our thoughts and our emotional response to any experience. This separation is similar to the experience of an athlete and his/her performance—the two are separate but aligned. From the athletic performance (object), the athlete (subject) can learn and make necessary adjustments; similarly, through observing thoughts and emotions, the self can learn and know itself.

Personal Reflections

Maslow argues that the lower hierarchy of needs must be met (physiological needs, safety, belongingness, esteem) before self-actualization can be realized. I proposed above that self-awareness and self-actualization go hand in hand. A technique that is widely practiced in organizational behavior to enhance self-awareness and personal development is the Johari Window model. It is often referred to as the disclosure/feedback model for self-awareness and is applied in a group setting. The Johari Window is composed of four panes of glass as follows:

Unknown by Self Unknown by Others	Unknown by Self Known by Others
Known by Self Unknown by Others	Known by Self Known by Others

Usually, the size of each pane is uneven (some are large, others small). Based on a series of questions and scenarios, the size of each pane can be determined for an individual. Through practice, the size of the panes can be changed. Ideally, the lower right-hand pane should be increased, the upper left-hand panes decreased. The Johari method is used in organizations and schools for personal development and group dynamics. The questions could be tailored, however, to make it an excellent tool for feedback on perceptions of individual members within a group—a list of appropriate questions is best left to a professional. The Know Me Game is based on the Johari Window model. You can find a reference at http://www.joharigame.com/.

What Does This Have to Do with Me?

A self-actualized individual is a fully functioning person who has reached the peak of his/her human potential. A self-actualized person is like a well-engineered car: so perfect in form that there is nothing better. Humanistic psychologists Carl Rogers and Abraham Maslow both emphasize that self-actualization represents the optimal psychological condition for all people. As I have argued, conscious awareness is a prerequisite for self-actualization. Much of what I have discussed throughout this book becomes the foundation for self-actualization.

A common saying is, "Life is full of experiences." We can learn much about our experiences by observing them from a point of reference called the experiencer. We put much faith into our experiences. We are told to experience life and all that it has to offer. Wise words, but much more can be gained from simply observing. We learn and grow from experience, but also through our own conscious awareness. We need to allow experience to be a window into the true self, a path to self-actualization.

You will find that through conscious awareness you will have more "aha" experiences, Eureka moments. During these times, you become aware of the essence of who you actually are and everything that you are capable of becoming.

Reality Check

For each statement below, write a "yes" or "no" answer in the rating column. When you are finished, add up the number of "yes" answers and record the total in the score row below.

Statement	Rating
1. Would you say that you are consciously aware of your thoughts?	_____
2. Do you understand how to be consciously aware of your thoughts?	_____
3. Had you heard about Maslow's concept of hierarchy of needs and self-actualization?	_____
4. Can you now differentiate between experiences and the experiencer? Try to write it down in words.	_____
5. Do you believe that conscious awareness could give you a better handle on self-actualization?	_____
Score (add up the "yes" answers, and write the sum)	_____

Interpretation

Ideally, you would write "yes" as an answer for each statement given. Attempt the "Things to Try" below.

Things to Try

1. The next time you hear, see, taste, smell, or feel something, take a brief moment to experience the sensation fully. Allow the sensation to permeate your body. Don't create internal labels for the sensation such as, "this food tastes great." Simply experience the sensation. Be present and allow the feeling to have its own space—allow it to expand and contract within you. As time progresses, allow the interval of time for awareness to increase.

2. Take two or three deep breaths, and feel the air coming through your nose into your lungs. Feel the body within. Repeat this a few times, and try to concentrate on your abdomen, chest, and upper body.

3. Try to become aware/conscious of your breathing at different times of the day: when walking, waiting for someone, sitting in a car or a bus.

4. Take five minutes during the day to have a quiet time by yourself. You may want to close your eyes. Visualize pleasant scenes or happy memories. Make this a habit.

Chapter 13

Taking Stock

The first nine chapters may have awakened us to:

- The unlimited potential that lies within
- The power of the present moment
- A true reality and how our mind-set creates illusions
- The state of effortless effort
- Right education and the importance of a positive attitude toward learning
- The timelessness domain and the peace that lies within

These earlier chapters have provided us with: a deeper understanding of how we learn and think; an appreciation of who we are; and an alternate way of looking at life.

The next three chapters applied the knowledge that we acquired and looked at sustainable life issues of health, relationships, self-fulfillment, and self-actualization.

In this chapter, we will take a ride to a vantage point and have a bird's-eye view of our past unconscious state, where we are now, and what is in store for us with our new mind-set. It will be the ride of our life, which leaves our past thoughts behind and provides an inkling of what we will soon become.

We can compare our journey in life to a ride on a Ferris wheel at an amusement park. We board the Ferris wheel, and slowly it moves up with some riders above us, and new riders who have come aboard below us. We eventually find ourselves alone, sitting on top of the world. A few anxious thoughts, perhaps. Our ascent until now has been slow. But of course that is not the reason we boarded the Ferris wheel. We wait in anticipation for the real ride to begin. The Ferris wheel turns and gradually picks up speed. At some point, we may lose focus on where we are. As we pick up more speed, the people on the ground are left behind and become blurs in the background. The wheel turns quickly, and we are immersed in the adventure, riding the outside of the Ferris wheel. We literally go along for the ride, since we have no control over it. The ride can be either exhilarating or frightening.

Imagine what would happen if we were to move closer to the center of the Ferris wheel. The impact of the ride would lessen. We would be consciously aware of everything that is happening on the Ferris wheel. We would feel more in control, and we would have a superb view of the surroundings. We would be on the inside looking out, and our enjoyment would be derived from within. At the center of the wheel, there is no anxiety, no waiting. It is more relaxing. We experience greater awareness of the situation and find joy in watching people on the ride.

Our mind-set is similar to the Ferris wheel. A mind that primarily places itself in the outer position, referred to as the ego, receives all the worldly benefits. Unfortunately, this typical mind-set is never satisfied and is always seeking more in order to feed its (ego) appetite. Move to the center and we find the inner self, which, we have learned, not only has all the power and control but contains within it a universal intelligence far superior to any egotistical mind. The outer view is what we have (content), the ego; the inner view is who we are (essence), egoless. Of course, we need balance between the two views. As on the Ferris wheel, at first we enjoy the thrill of the ride. We experience life. Then, as we become aware of an alternate position, at the center of the wheel, we find an inner reality. Eventually, we will rely more on our inner being, as we come to realize its importance and potential.

Initially, finding our essence and balancing the outer with the inner view will be difficult. As with the Ferris wheel, once we have felt the exhilaration, we want it to continue. Like a spoiled child who steadfastly refuses to get off the ride, our old mind-set believes that we have to hold on to what we have. With practice, though, and balancing our outer and inner reality, everything we feel, think, do, and say will be brought into harmony with the oneness of life.

All this might sound complex, but really it is not. Stripping away the layers conjured by the mind leaves only one basic question that we need to answer. Whatever problems we have, we need to first answer the question, "Who am I, really?" Once we know this truthfully and deeply, the light within will dissolve the darkness of all our worries and doubts.

Chapter 14

The New You

The "new you" is you experiencing life in the present moment. Let us revisit and summarize our understanding of the present moment.

Psychologically speaking, the present moment is all that we have. The past and the future only have meaning because we are thinking of them in the present. We would be far better off if we could live life solely in the present moment. In the words of psychotherapist Carl Rogers: "An increasing tendency to live fully in each moment. Consequently such a person would realize that, 'What I will be in the next moment, and what I will do, grows out of that moment.'"[1] Complete attention to the present moment is by no means easy. Attention requires a high degree of alertness. The more we are aware, the more we have control of our actions and feelings. Does the following ring true? "My work is mundane. The only way I survive the day is by thinking of what I will be doing on my upcoming holidays." Is this not an escape, a reality based on an unknown future? The person is a thousand miles away from what s/he is doing, thinking of some future activity, unaware of the present moment. A wall has been built between the self and the present.

How, then, can we awake from this dreamlike state? We dream because we are not focusing on what we are doing, thinking instead of a reality that has either already taken place (past) or is yet to happen (future). If we spend most of our time contemplating what happened in the past or dreaming about what may happen in the future, then we are missing what is occurring at this very instant in time.

How different is our normal daily unconscious state from our nighttime sleeping state? Probably not much; either way, we do a great deal of dreaming. Would it not be better to awaken from our daytime dreamlike state? This awakening will require a drastic shift in our mind-set. We will need to shake off the unconscious and reside in the present moment.

Attaining the "new you" requires moving through three stages: accepting the "what is" condition, developing an awareness of presence, and surrendering completely to the present moment. Let's elaborate further.

Stage One: accept the fact that we are unaware of the internal dialogue that takes place in our head, and admit that this dialogue is completely out of our control.

The Buddhists' term for this state is monkey mind. A mind that chatters incessantly swings from self-doubt to worry and back to doubt again; and from the past to the future and back again. Our monkey mind is different in content but similar in tone to other people's monkey minds. It "appears logical, even seductive, but also cunning, baffling and powerful."[2]

If we listen to our monkey mind carefully, we will find that most of the dialogue deals with thinking about past or future events—responding defensively to negative comments, positively when the ego is stroked; comparing the self with others; justifying what can't be done; complaining about other people and situations; making excuses. When we analyze this list, we conclude that most of the thoughts have little purpose.

Stage Two: identify techniques that will enhance our awareness and help us focus on the "present moment."

We all have a monkey mind; how do we change it to a human mind—one that is focused, alert, under control? Well, we could pay attention to all the dialogue that is taking place in our mind. This would not be easy. Approximately 60,000 thoughts pass through our mind every day. To be alert and take control of these thoughts would be an impossible task. Instead, we will construct some speed bumps, so to speak, that will slow down the mind and allow us to control it.

Researchers have proven that we are more aware of our thoughts during quiet times. Times when we are by ourselves, such as waiting for a bus or a friend, getting ready for school or work in the morning, sitting alone. We are alone many times during the day. So, here is the first speed bump we can try. During these quiet times, focus on the thoughts that enter the mind—listen to our personal monkey. Initially, the process will be a complete surprise. "Wow, I didn't realize that I was thinking internally." "My goodness, I have a monkey mind." These observations are the beginning of awareness. Under no circumstances try to stop the monkey mind from chattering. Over time, just being aware of the monkey mind will slow down the internal chattering. This slowing down is akin to a train with many carriages, which initially is moving so fast nothing is discernible. Then, after a while, the train slows down just a little. Now we notice it is a passenger train, and we see people moving about the train. Later, as we continue to observe, the train appears even slower, and we are aware that some of the passengers are reading, others eating, some are talking, sitting, or playing games. Eventually, the train almost stops, and now our awareness is so keen that we observe most everything that is happening on the train.

So simple, so effective; just by observing the mind, uncontrollable thoughts cease to occur. Be careful. We are not suggesting that thinking will stop altogether, merely that the monkey mind is now under our power. Over time, we will find that the monkey responds and respects our determination to control. With this newfound power, we observe many changes. We will become more alert, possess more energy, have less stress and better health, and improve our coping skills.

The next speed bump is huge and well documented. The speed bump has been known for over 2,500 years and was passed down to us by the wise sages. The speed bump stands alone as the best means of attaining conscious awareness, presence, and peacefulness. The speed bump we will talk about is meditation. The principles involved in meditation are timeless and when employed correctly, work immediately. Meditation applies to all religions or none, belongs to no culture or beliefs, and it has an appeal to all.

For our purpose, we will use a meditative process by directing our attention to some specific word or phrase. The process we will mention is only one of many described in books and other literature on meditation. We will observe our thoughts closely, shift our focus of attention away from our usual thoughts, and repeat a mantra. The difference between this method and the one we described earlier is that we find a specific time during the day to practice awareness. The best times are first thing every morning before we start our day and in the evening just before we retire.

A mantra is a systematic repetition of a word, phrase, verse, or saying. We know the importance of physical exercise, and the beneficial effect it has on the body. Meditation is an exercise for the mind. "Meditation is a cleansing of the glass so that when we look at it we see right through it."[3] What is the purpose of a mantra? Why do we need to choose a mantra? A lovely allegory from the writings of Eknath Easwaran (paraphrased for the sake of brevity) follows:

On festival days in India you will see huge elephants adorned in gold and gorgeous cloth. Everyone enjoys the sight. But there is one difficulty. Stalls of fruit and vegetables and sweets line the narrow streets, and the trunk of the elephant rarely stays still. It is always swaying back and forth, up and down. So, as the procession comes abreast of a fruit stall, the elephant seizes a coconut or a bunch of bananas. The fruit vendors cannot afford this kind of loss. To prevent it, the mahout asks the elephant to grasp a firm stick in his trunk. Holding the bamboo stick in his trunk, the elephant steps right along, not tempted by the mangoes or melons because he has something to hold on to.[4]

The human mind is rather like the trunk of an elephant. It never rests, is forever wandering here and there. Occasionally the mind is useful in solving a problem, or making plans, but most of the time it wanders unnecessarily because we do not know how to keep it quiet.

When we meditate, the mantra is the stick that the elephant holds in his mouth. Faithfully repeat the mantra every day at the same time for about twenty minutes. When repeating the mantra, don't succumb to the temptation of dozing off, or holding on to a thought that is pleasing. Through concentration and the repetition of a word, phrase, or saying, thoughts will cease to enter the mind. Be silent and peaceful, and through this commitment, a strong relationship with the universe will be formed. In the words of Thomas Keating: "Silence is a language that God speaks, and everything else is a bad translation."

Repeating a mantra sounds too simple, and many might question its usefulness. Some people would argue that it is a mere mechanical repetition for which a recorder could do a better job. Those who argue for a recorder fail to understand the essence of meditation.

By our repeating a mantra, that which cannot be understood will be understood, and that which cannot be seen will be seen. Mahatma Gandhi said, "The mantra becomes one's staff of life. It is not repeated for the sake of repetition, but for the sake of purification."

Selecting a mantra that is just right takes careful planning. If you are religious at all, choose an ancient saying or script that contains spiritual meaning. Once you have selected a mantra, do not change it. "Well, it just isn't doing what it's supposed to do," is often said as an excuse to change. This argument from the old mind-set is wrong. Keep your mantra, and never change it. With the chosen mantra, state explicitly its intention, believe in it with unwavering faith, visualize the stillness and peace that it will bring.

Although meditation is the ultimate speed bump for awareness and mind control, there are other ways of slowing down the monkey mind. Some other noteworthy speed bumps that we can incorporate include: slowing down, one-pointed attention, training the senses, putting others first, spiritual companionship, reading the mystics. Each one of these speed bumps is highly recommended. Some are easy to implement. For example, try to eat more slowly, and organize the day so there is time to read a book for relaxation. Consider the importance of family and friends. Relax, enjoy their company, and give them the time they deserve. Read the reference material mentioned in this book and recommended in the reference section.

A dictum for our modern-day society is, "Work hard and success will surely follow." Like robots, we start our day on automatic pilot, and for the rest of the day it is hurry, go fast, even faster, don't stop. Deviate from society's wishes, and adopt a new dictum, "I have no time to be in a hurry."

Stage Three: Our final goal is to change our mind-set so completely that we find we are fully aware of most every moment.

The question is, "Can this stage ever be achieved?" And to a degree it can. What is the benchmark? Some mystics argue that the goal of complete conscious awareness and living in the present moment is reserved for the enlightened few. There are degrees of success, however, and the fun is to try, without knowing what level of competence we will achieve.

Of course, our mind is not fully aware of every moment; otherwise, we would not be reading this book. Let us explain, however, how we can go beyond Stage Two, and then identify the ultimate outcome for Stage Three.

Earlier we mentioned that the best time to practice awareness is during quiet moments (Stage Two). Of course, with our busy schedules, time is limited. Quiet times, however, are not restricted to periods when we are alone. If we listen, the silence around us will awaken stillness within us. For example, the observation of nature will invoke stillness, even if people and other activities are all around us. Any outer noise can also bring about stillness. Simply accept the noise. Don't resist it, and your inner self will find peace. Philosophers and mystics speak about the space between the words. Between every spoken word is a lapse in time when nothing is said. Silence is in the lapse. For example, when I listened to the Dalai Lama just recently, the peace that he mentioned occurred between his spoken words.

Some of the more contemporary teachers describe the final outcome as follows. Eckhart Tolle calls it "awakened doing," Krishnamurti refers to it as "awakened intelligence," Buddhism and the Dalai Lama speak of "spiritual enlightenment," Rollo May says it is the "creative consciousness of self," Abraham Maslow terms it "self-actualization." The message is the same, though the words are different. If we can achieve this result, we have reached the highest level of human potential. Some even suggest we will have found the ultimate human purpose.

We need to explain the final outcome in the context of what has been presented in this book. We have toyed with the notion that our mind-set is not only "out of control" but also conditioned by the past. We are conditioned by the whole of humanity, and influenced by the beliefs, culture, and norms of society. We need to find peace, truth, in order to find ourselves. In our present state of being, we are unable to do this.

Krishnamurti spoke of "setting every living person free," psychologically speaking. Rollo May suggests that we need the "courage to be one's self." The courage to find out who we are and change what is not right. In order to be "what we were always meant to be," we need a paradigm shift—a change in our mind-set. The first twelve chapters of the book explain how this is possible. Each chapter opens a window to the inner self, which will ultimately liberate our conscious being and set us free.

In summary, here are some suggestions:

- Accept "what is" at the external level, and be aware of an inner self.
- Adopt a mantra, and practice meditation.
- Give full attention to the present moment.
- Slow down.
- Be aware of the space between words; breathing, thinking.
- Allow the being to be part of the doing.

How can we put this into practice? Read Appendix C: A Prescription for Happiness.

Chapter 15

So What's Next?

"Who are You?" crooned the Caterpillar.
Alice replied rather shyly,
"I—I hardly know, Sir, just at present.
I know who I was when I got up this morning,
But I think I must have changed several times since then."

—Lewis Carroll, *Alice in Wonderland*

The previous chapters have taken us on a journey into the inner self and laid the foundation for a new way of thinking that will eventually change who we are into what we were always meant to be. A transformation of the self is already taking place within us; we see things differently as a universal being; our purpose and promise of a better future is now ready to unfold. Let us go back to the beginning and explore what we have accomplished on this journey into the self.

We began with the premise that the old ways of solving human problems are not working and are in need of a change. We suggested that the old ways were based on a mind-set of working from the outside-in; an intellectual mind used to resolve our issues and worries. We then introduced the concept of a new inside-out mind-set, one that works from within and utilizes a universal intelligence. The book suggests that the path toward this intelligence is through conscious awareness. Conscious awareness can be thought of as a point of focus where all our energies are concentrated. Like a lens used to direct light to a centricity, the mind has an intense power when focused to a single point. In our discussions, conscious awareness is our single point of concentration, and with it a very powerful force is unleashed. Initially, meditation is used to direct the mind to a single point of attention.

In exploring the twelve paradigms discussed in this book, I hope your view of life has changed. I expect you have recognized the importance of a paradigm shift—a change from a limited mind-set to a universal mind-set with the promise that we can accomplish all that we attempt. Recall that these paradigms were arbitrarily selected; we could substitute others, particularly any life obstacles we want to overcome. The importance of the paradigm is not in the achievement of concrete goals but in effecting change in how we feel and think. As an example, I mentioned in chapter 1 that anything we give from the heart will be returned to us in abundance in different ways. Not in the form of money or material wealth, but rather in psychological and emotional benefits, such as joy in what we do, positive feedback from others, deeper friendships, recognition, happiness, a purpose in being, and better health. In our journey to the inner self, we have reached the summit, satisfied that we have accomplished more than we ever thought possible. Let us briefly revisit the twelve paradigms in sequence to take a panoramic view of our journey.

Abundance We were introduced to the potential wealth that lies within every person. The means is easy to understand. Simply, "Become more aware, moment by moment, of what is happening around us." This is an essential step toward conscious awareness as it relates to the physical, emotional, and spiritual aspects of our life.

Completeness We learned that every person is part of the whole. The old mind-set limits and separates us from the whole by race, culture, religion, color, status, and position. The new mind-set, however, has a holistic view that unifies all of humanity based on actions, deeds, and a spiritual reverence for life.

Presence Chapter 3 talks about living in the present moment. Most daily rituals are an act of doing. To live presence, we need to recognize that there are dual forces at work: doing and thinking. What we do invokes the present moment, but what we are thinking often has little to do with the present moment. The antidote is to become aware of what we are thinking. The chapter suggested a number of techniques to try.

Intention Here we delve into the state of doing and being. Most people are doers; fewer are involved with being. The suggestion was to integrate the being with the doing. If our intention is primarily being, then the doing will arise naturally, effortlessly, lovingly, joyfully.

Reality Our perception of reality varies from person to person. Sages tell us that our best view of reality is achieved when we focus all our attention on each and every moment.

Effort Effort for some is laborious, difficult, tiring. Others find effort enjoyable, rewarding, motivating. It is all a matter of attitude. Accept what is, be completely involved, and identify the positive aspects of the task.

Learning Learning requires that we take responsibility, have a positive attitude and an open mind, accept what needs to be done, be fully involved.

Mind Control Mindfulness is the art of staying in the present moment, a means of being, staying focused with positive thoughts.

As when we are driving a car, we must take control of our mind. The key to mind control is being aware and attending to our thoughts. We learned that what we think is who we are.

Time Two concepts of time were introduced: clock time and psychological time. Clock time is welded to the doing part of life. Psychological time or timelessness is the universal mind-set, an integral part of our being. We are asked to be aware and work in both dimensions of time.

Health Our body is our temple—treat it with respect and take good care of it. The power of positive thinking was introduced and how it has a major influence on our health. Brainswitching is an excellent technique for turning negative thoughts into positive ones.

Relationships Such an important topic for youth. Too many of us take from a relationship and give little in return. The main cause of a poor relationship is the ego. The lesson in this chapter is that when you give unconditionally, you usually receive much more in return.

Self-Actualization Self-actualization is the realization of one's potential. To realize our full potential, we need to understand the self. The way to achieve this is through conscious awareness. We learn the importance of separating experiences from the experiencer, and why this is another path to conscious awareness.

Recall that the principal purpose of the twelve paradigms was conscious awareness, and the desired outcome of each paradigm is the change of a limited mind-set into a universal mind-set. Even the Buddha, when asked what made him different, responded, "I am aware of my thoughts." Conscious awareness is a coming out of the self, a means of turning the self inside out.

Those who have applied the concepts presented in this book find varied results. For some, conscious awareness is immediate;

it is as if they have come from a dreamlike state into an awakened-life state in one brief moment. For others, it is a slower process of acceptance, then clarity, then psychological well-being, then complete awareness. In either situation, the reaction is the same—a truly amazing journey of self-discovery. Understand, though, that neither this book nor any other authority can unlock the door to conscious awareness, although many people may say otherwise. This book is simply a road map, a route to travel. It is up to each one of us individually to take the initiative.

Now that we have scaled the mountain, reached the summit, what is next? We may feel this book has been just one mountain, the beginning of many other mountains to climb. And I agree. But don't be disheartened; take solace in the knowledge that, as we scale new mountains, we become even more skilled in our practice of conscious awareness. We can draw on the writings of sages who have themselves traversed mountains. Personally, I never tire of reading these enlightening books. The first book I read on the subject was Krishnamurti's *Commentaries on Living* series. I spent many hours reading not one, but eventually all, of Krishnamurti's books. Every word, every page, spoke volumes to me. Books like *Commentaries on Living* are meant to inspire us, explain how we can change, guide us toward a more meaningful life. But no matter how many books we read, we will not change without practicing the teachings. A student of mine proudly admitted that she had read over one hundred books on meditation and spirituality. When I asked how successful she was at meditating, she admitted that she was too busy reading and studying and had not found the time to practice meditation yet. Meditating is an important step toward conscious awareness. It may be difficult to assimilate all the concepts in this book and others, but do not continue reading without taking the first, most important, step. Try meditation. Many people find that reading a chapter of Krishnamurti or Tolle or any other of the authors mentioned in the bibliography, just before bedtime, relaxes them. They then silently repeat their mantra, which further soothes the mind until sleep takes hold. This technique is highly effective because what we put in the mind just prior to sleeping stays in the unconscious mind through our sleeping time. We find that, with continuous practice, awareness becomes possible. It may be slow at first, but, after a few bumps, the pace accelerates.

Now that we have come to the end of this book, we realize that our journey together is but the beginning of another. We have scaled the peaks of conscious awareness and self-understanding. For those who continue the journey, may you find all that you are seeking. For those who want to rest awhile: hold on to the vision, and when the light illuminates your path, may you continue on with the quest. And to all: our journey has taken us where few have gone before. We have discovered new worlds, a new way of thinking, and transformed ourselves from simply being who we are into what we were always meant to be.

Appendix A

A Living Document

Quite possibly the material that was presented in this book is more important than anything else that you can think of, or do, or read. Just consider—this book will help you discover who you really are; and what can be more important, more exciting, than self-discovery? Read the book often, and put it down even more often, but always remember where it is, so that you can reread it. Think of the many practical ways this book can affect your life; plan and implement a strategy. Add your own ideas, take away those concepts that you don't like, discuss the ideas with your friends, share your thoughts.

A Web site in the form of a blog is available with this book. The blog is located at http://turningselfinsideout.blogspot.com/. If you are unfamiliar with blogging, visit http://codex.wordpress.org/Introduction_to_Blogging. Specific information about my blog can be found at: https://www.blogger.com/. In a few words, a blog is a publication of personal thoughts or comments about an area of interest (in my case, the book) which can be viewed and shared by other members who sign into the blog.

The blog is fun, easy to use, and adds further value to the material presented in this book. If you have a comment or idea or just want to talk to other people who have read the book, log on to the blog at http://turningselfinsideout.blogspot.com/, and do a posting to the site.

Blogs are usually short discourses: brief thoughts or ideas or suggestions. If you are interested in making a longer submission, you can contribute to our e-newsletter by sending an e-mail to: turningselfinsideout@gmail.com. In the subject header of the e-mail, write "Newsletter Contribution." To subscribe, use the same e-mail address as above, and in the subject header write "Subscribe."

Appendix B

Your Life Satisfaction Rating

Are you satisfied with your life? Are you generally a happy person? Try the following and find out where you rank.

Below are five statements with which you may agree or disagree. Using the scale below, indicate your agreement or disagreement with each item by placing the appropriate number in the box under rating. Please be open and honest in your response.

7 Strongly agree

6 Agree

5 Slightly agree

4 Neither agree nor disagree

3 Slightly disagree

2 Disagree

1 Strongly disagree

Statement	Rating (1 to 7)
In most ways my life is close to ideal.	_____
The conditions of my life are excellent.	_____
I am satisfied with my life.	_____

So far I have attained the important things I want in life. _____

If I could live my life over, I would change almost nothing. _____

Add up the numbers and write the sum here: _____

Interpretation

☐ 31–35	Extremely satisfied
☐ 26–30	Satisfied
☐ 21–25	Slightly satisfied
☐ 20	Neutral
☐ 15–19	Slightly dissatisfied
☐ 10–14	Dissatisfied
☐ 5–9	Extremely dissatisfied

Understanding Scores on the Satisfaction Life Scale

Author: Ed Diener Phd, Psychologist

30-35 Very high score; highly satisfied

Respondents who score in this range love their lives and feel that things are going very well. Their lives are not perfect, but they feel that things are about as good as life gets. Furthermore, just because the person is satisfied does not mean he is complacent. In fact, growth and challenge might be part of the reason the respondent is satisfied. For most people in this high-scoring range, life is enjoyable, and the major domains of life are going well—work or school, family, friends, leisure, and personal development.

25-29 High score

Individuals who score in this range like their lives and feel that things are going well. Of course their lives are not perfect, but they feel that things are mostly good. Furthermore, just because the person is satisfied does not mean he is complacent. In fact, growth and challenge might be part of the reason the respondent is satisfied. For most people in this high-scoring range, life is enjoyable, and the major domains of life are going well—work or school, family, friends, leisure, and personal development. The person may draw motivation from the areas of dissatisfaction.

20-24 Average score

The average of life satisfaction in economically developed nations is in this range—the majority of people are generally satisfied, but have some areas where they very much would like some improvement. Some individuals score in this range because they are mostly satisfied with most areas of their lives but see the need for some improvement in each area. Other respondents score in this range because they are satisfied with most domains of their lives, but have one or two areas where they would like to see large improvements. A person scoring in this range is normal in that they have areas of their lives that need improvement. However, an individual in this range would usually like to move to a higher level by making some life changes.

15-19 Slightly below average in life satisfaction

People who score in this range usually have small but significant problems in several areas of their lives, or have many areas that are doing fine but one area that represents a substantial problem for them. If a person has moved temporarily into this level of life satisfaction from a higher level because of some recent event, things will usually improve over time and satisfaction will generally move back up. On the other hand, if a person is chronically slightly dissatisfied with many areas of life, some changes might be in order. Sometimes the person is simply expecting too much, and sometimes life changes are needed. Thus, although temporary dissatisfaction is common and normal, a chronic level of dissatisfaction across a number of areas of life calls for reflection. Some people can gain motivation from a small level of dissatisfaction, but often dissatisfaction across a number of life domains is a distraction, and unpleasant as well.

10-14 Dissatisfied

People who score in this range are substantially dissatisfied with their lives. People in this range may have a number of domains that are not going well, or one or two domains that are going very badly. If life dissatisfaction is a response to a recent event such as bereavement, divorce, or a significant problem at work, the person will probably return over time to his or her former level of higher satisfaction. However, if low levels of life satisfaction have been chronic for the person, some changes are in order—both in attitudes and patterns of thinking, and probably in life activities as well. Low levels of life satisfaction in this range, if they persist, can indicate that things are going badly and life alterations are needed. Furthermore, a person with low life satisfaction in this range is sometimes not functioning well because their unhappiness serves as a distraction. Talking to a friend, member of the clergy, counselor, or other specialist can often help the person get moving in the right direction, although positive change will be up to the person.

5-9 Extremely Dissatisfied

Individuals who score in this range are usually extremely unhappy with their current life. In some cases this is in reaction to some recent bad event such as failure or unemployment. In other cases, it is a response to a chronic problem such as alcoholism, drugs or addiction. In yet other cases the extreme dissatisfaction is a reaction due to something bad in life such as recently having lost a loved one. However, dissatisfaction at this level is often due to dissatisfaction in multiple areas of life. Whatever the reason for the low level of life satisfaction, it may be that the help of others is needed—a friend or family member, counseling with a member of the clergy, or help from a psychologist or other counselor. If the dissatisfaction is chronic, the person needs to change, and often others can help.

Part that is common to each category

To understand life satisfaction scores, it is helpful to understand some of the components that go into most people's experience of satisfaction. One of the most important influences on happiness is social relationships. People who score high on life satisfaction tend to have close and supportive family and friends, whereas those who do not have close friends and family are more likely to be dissatisfied. Of course, the loss of a close friend or family member can cause dissatisfaction with life, and it may take quite a time for the person to bounce back from the loss.

Another factor that influences the life satisfaction of most people is work or school, or performance in an important role such as homemaker or parent. When the person enjoys his or her work, whether it is paid or unpaid work, and feels that it is meaningful and important, this contributes to life satisfaction. When work is going poorly because of bad circumstances or a poor fit with the person's strengths, this can lower life satisfaction. When a person has important goals and is failing to make adequate progress toward them, this too can lead to life dissatisfaction.

A third factor that influences the life satisfaction of most people is personal satisfaction with the self, religious or spiritual life, learning and growth, and leisure. For many people these are sources of satisfaction. However, when these sources of personal worth are frustrated, they can be powerful sources of dissatisfaction. Of course there are additional sources of satisfaction and dissatisfaction – some that are common to most people such as health, and others that are unique to each individual. Most people know the factors that lead to their satisfaction or dissatisfaction, although a person's temperament, a general tendency to be happy or unhappy, can color their responses.

There is no one key to life satisfaction, but rather a recipe that includes a number of ingredients. With time and persistent work, people's life satisfaction usually goes up when they are dissatisfied. People who have had a loss recover over time. People who have a dissatisfying relationship or work environment often make changes over time that will increase their satisfaction. One key ingredient to happiness, as mentioned above, is social relationships, and another key ingredient is to have important goals that derive from one's values, and to make progress toward those goals. For many people it is important to feel a connection to something larger than oneself. When a person tends to be chronically dissatisfied, they should **look within themselves** and ask whether they need to develop more **positive attitudes** to life and the world.

Copyright by Ed Diener, February 13, 2006

For more information, go to: http://www.psych.uiuc.edu/~ediener/SWLS.htm

Use is free of charge and granted by permission.

Appendix C

Prescription for Happiness

This appendix details a process for improving conscious awareness—a prescription for happiness. This appendix will be most useful if you have completed the first fourteen chapters of the book.

Here is a four-step process for improving conscious awareness. Each step is correlated numerically by section.

Section 1: Improve Your Conscious Awareness

    1.   Meditate (concentrate on your breath, or an object, or repeat your mantra).

    2.   Focus on your mind and become attentive.

    3.   Acquire presence and take more control of your life.

    4.   Switch from the outside-in to the inside-out philosophy and observe life from within.

Section 2: Apply Conscious Awareness to Your Daily Living

    1.   Meditate for twenty minutes, particularly in the early morning and late at night.

    2.   Pay attention to your monkey mind during quiet times: waiting, riding on a bus or train, bathing, brushing your teeth or hair, relaxing.

3. Interrupt briefly any repetitive, engaging activity and listen to the mental noise within. Interrupt while: eating, working, studying, gardening, running, reading a book, playing a game, washing dishes, doing laundry.

4. Observe your interactions during the day with people, animals, Nature, and the environment.

Section 3: Recognize the State of Conscious Awareness

Once you have achieved this state you will:

1. Feel a sense of peacefulness and awareness during meditation.

2. Feel a sense of peacefulness and awareness during quiet times.

3. Experience an immediate sense of awareness and joy when you interrupt a repetitive task.

4. Experience a sense of communal oneness, compassion, joy, and enthusiasm in all your interactions.

Each day, follow the recommended processes to improve your conscious awareness. The outcomes mentioned under Recognize the State of Conscious Awareness may not be achieved immediately. Perhaps you will find a sense of peacefulness only during meditation, but have difficulty experiencing a state of joy and communal oneness when speaking with co-workers. Continue the practice, and don't worry about the results. Be patient with yourself, commit to a daily practice, not just for yourself, but for all.

Helpful Suggestions

You are stretched in all directions. You want to accomplish so much in a day, but find you have too little time to complete everything. Even so, take time to commit to your morning meditation. Set your alarm ten minutes earlier the first week, and then add an additional ten minutes the second week. When the alarm rings, repeat internally, "Starting off every day with my meditation is the most important thing I can do for myself, and through meditation I will find peace and happiness in my life." Memorize this short statement and repeat it every morning when you first wake. Start your meditation process as soon as you are fully awake. Slowly increase the duration, ideally to twenty minutes, but no more than thirty minutes.

Now that you have committed to a morning ritual, you are ready to apply conscious awareness in your daily schedule. Identify times during the day when you have downtime—time when you are alone. Write down each situation and the ideal times when you have downtime: walking to or from the parking lot, during coffee breaks, when stretching to relieve tension, walking for exercise, traveling by bus, waiting for someone. For each situation, approximate the duration of the downtime—in total it should last twenty to forty-five minutes each day. Use these downtimes to become familiar with your monkey mind. Attending to your monkey mind allows you to expand and integrate conscious awareness into your daily routine. Slowly, you become aware of the chatter from your monkey. Do not chastise or become upset with your monkey. Simply focus on the noise made by your monkey. Awareness is a powerful tool that leads to complete attention of the mind. Periodically review the list that you created for downtimes, and if possible add to the list.

Next, identify specific times when you can practice conscious awareness while doing an activity. Do not attempt this technique when you are involved in a dangerous activity, such as driving a car, climbing a mountain, or operating machinery. Examples of appropriate activities include: when listening to a speaker, during a long meeting, or when studying, gardening, ironing, or reading an annual report. Stop what you are doing for a brief moment, at a convenient time, and observe the mind. These moments are called interrupts. Use interrupts during times when there are lapses in the activity, or times when you need to refocus. Start with a few interrupts, and gradually increase the number over time. Do not use interrupts as an excuse to escape from what you are doing, but instead use interrupts to pause your thinking. Identify situations where you can introduce an interrupt, and tabulate a list. Thirty or fewer daily interrupts is a suitable number.

The final suggestion is based on your personal interactions. For example: talking with friends, communicating with colleagues, spending time with your pet, observing the beauty of Nature, feeling the breeze on your face. For these spontaneous interactions, observe your reaction. Initially, you may find that there is a gap between the time when the event took place and your observation. This gap is normal, as in: "I realized somewhat later that I felt a breeze on my face," or, "The awareness of how upset I felt occurred to me much later." The gap between the event and the awareness will decrease over time. Eventually you may be aware at the very moment the event occurs. How often should you be fully immersed in the present moment? This awareness should be your modus operandi at all times—when the observer and the observed become one.

Reflect on what you learned from this appendix. Do you believe it is a prescription for happiness? There is strong supporting evidence from many sources: quantum physics, medicine, psychology and psychiatry, and education suggesting that this prescription works. So, apply the four-step process and be happy. Write down the following Web site address: http://blip.tv/file/336766 and type the URL into your favourite search engine. The Web site contains a wonderful twenty-six-minute audio on Steps to a Balanced Life—an inspiring summary of many of the concepts presented in both this book and appendix.

Appendix D

Glossary of Terms

AA Acronym for Alcoholics Anonymous, which is an informal, worldwide society whose primary purpose is to help its members stay sober and abstain from alcohol.

Affective Domain In education, this includes motivation, values, attitudes, feelings, awareness. It is often contrasted with the cognitive domain, which includes the acquisition of knowledge.

Being Most philosophers would argue that "being" cannot be defined, or at least that it is open to many definitions. In this book, however, we distinguish an inner self (being) from an outer mind (thinking). Other terms that are similar in concept include: the soul, the heart, higher self, God within, Atman, spirit.

Blog (short for Web blog) A chronological publication of personal thoughts on a particular subject of interest. Since a blog is a type of Web site, and is therefore not restricted to text, it may also include images, links, data, and other media objects.

Consciousness The awareness of mental processes, not the processes themselves. There are three philosophical positions on consciousness: that it is supernatural (unnatural phenomenon; cannot be understood); that it is a natural phenomenon (occurs naturally; cannot be understood); that it is a brain function (can be understood).[1]

Essentialism/perennialism/progressivism The three pillars of education used to describe the philosophies of the learning process. These philosophies focus on what we should teach—the curriculum aspect. Essentialism emphasizes "back to basics theory"; perennialism identifies a common nature leading to the discovery of truth and logical choices; progressivism encourages initiative, creativity, and self-expression, and is the basis of holistic education.

Eureka moment The term attributed to Archimedes when he stepped from his bathtub and realized that the water level had dropped. His response was, *Eureka,* when he discovered, quite by accident, that the volume of water displaced was equivalent to the volume of his body. A moment of genius.

Holistic education A philosophy of education based on the premise that each person finds identity, meaning, and purpose in life through connections to the community, to the natural world, and to spiritual values.

Humanistic education Emphasizes the whole person, not just the intellect, and is concerned with the growth and development that are the signs of real learning. Many of the theories and practices evolved from humanistic psychology.

Intelligence A person's ability to learn and remember information, to recognize concepts and their relations, and to apply the information to his or her own behavior in an adaptive way.

MADD Acronym for Mothers against Drunk Driving. A nonprofit anti-alcohol advocacy organization with chapters in Canada and the United States.

Mantra Literally translated as "a place to rest the mind." It is a sacred syllable, poem, prayer, or sound that is repeated during meditation. Mantra meditation predates Buddhism.

Mindfulness An ability to sustain continuous attention, an awareness of the present moment. Mindfulness is an activity that can be done at any time, as in, mindful of our feet when walking. Indirectly, it is a form of meditation.

Mind-set The term can be defined as a person's frame of reference. In the book, I have identified two types of mind-sets: limiting and universal. A person can have a particular mind-set that is so set in a specific outlook that s/he does not see other perspectives. This prevents looking at new options in a realistic sense. A mind that is set or fixed is limiting; in contrast, a mind that is not fixed is open to universal thoughts and concepts.

Perception A rapid, automatic, unconscious process by which we recognize what is represented by the information provided by our sense organs. [2]

Right education This is all about educating the whole person: the mind, the body, and the soul. Educational institutions emphasize intellectual capacity and encourage excellence in academic studies. But what about learning how to: Find freedom from self-centered action and inner conflict? Discover the self and what right livelihood means? To find clarity from a sense of order and valuing the inner self?

Social engineering A concept that refers to efforts to influence popular attitudes and social behavior on a large scale, whether by governments or private groups. It has become prolific through the Internet, for example, with pop-ups, advertisements, and e-mails.

SWOT or SWOT Analysis is a planning tool used to evaluate the Strengths, Weaknesses, Opportunities, and Threats involved in a business context. It can also be applied personally to help you develop your career in a way that takes best advantage of your talents, abilities, and opportunities. It involves specifying your objectives and identifying the internal and external factors that are favorable and unfavorable to achieving those objectives.

Universal intelligence There is more to intelligence than human intelligence. Universal intelligence is a term used to describe what we see as organization, or order, in the universe. It is self-evident that new knowledge can have no meaning unless we already know how to interpret it. Our ability to analyze massive amounts of always changing, almost random information bombarding our senses at the speed of light demonstrates that something magnificent is occurring within our minds. What this means is that our conscious mind is in communication with a subconscious mind that already knows what to do. It also means that the universe is in communication with our subconscious minds. The universe sends us information for which we must already know the meaning. Our universal intelligence contains the meaning of the universe.

Upanishads The word literally means "sitting down near" and implies studying with a spiritual teacher. The Upanishads were written by Indian sages between the eighth and fourth centuries BC.

Notes

Author's Notes
1. Palmer, *The Courage to Teach*, 4.

Introduction
1. Wilbur, *Sex, Ecology, Spirituality*, 3.

Prologue
1. *The American Heritage Dictionary of the English Language*, 4th ed. Boston: Houghton Mifflin Company, 2004), http://dictionary.reference.com/browse/paradigm (accessed July 30, 2008).

Chapter 1
1. Easwaran, *Meditation: A Simple Eight-Point Program*, 19.

2. "Write Spirit, Mother Teresa Quotes." http://www.writespirit.net/authors/mother_teresa/mother_teresa_quotes/mother_teresa_love (accessed November 15, 2007).

3. Rogers, *On Becoming a Person*, 115–118.

Chapter 2
1. "On Truth & Reality: The Spherical Standing Wave Structure of Matter (WSM) in Space." Quoted in http://www.

spaceandmotion.com/ (accessed January 10, 2008).

2. The Institute of Noetic Sciences. "About Ions." Quoted in http://www.noetic.org/about/founder.cfm (accessed February 1, 2008).

Chapter 3

1. Helmsletter, *What to Say When You Talk to Yourself,* inside front matter.

Chapter 4

1. Trump, *Trump 101,* inside front matter.

2. Gratzon, *The Lazy Way to Success*, 24.

3. Oliner, *The Altruistic Personality: Rescuers of Jews in Nazi Germany,* 1–5.

4. Englishclub.com, ESL Forums. "Talking Point, September 2007." http://www.englishclub.com/esl-forums/viewtopic.php?t=46409 (accessed January 15, 2008).

5. US Department of Labor, Bureau of Labor Statistics. "Overview of Report on the American Workforce." http://www.bls.gov/opub/rtaw/rtawhome.htm (accessed January 15, 2008).

Chapter 5

1. Findlaw, Legal News and Commentary. "How Reliable is Eyewitness Testimony?: A Decision by New York State's Highest Court Reveals Unsettling Truths about Juries." http://writ.news.findlaw.com/dorf/20010516.html (accessed December 10, 2007).

2. Quoted in http://sarvamekam.wordpress.com/2007/12/03/rational-vs-rationalizing/ (accessed December 14, 2007).

Chapter 6
1. Csikszentmihalyi, *Flow: The Psychology of Optimal Experience*, 108.

Chapter 8
1. Easwaran, *Meditation: A Simple Eight-Point Program*, 21.

2. deMello, *Awareness: The Perils and Opportunities of Reality*, Foreword.

3. Byrne, *The Secret*, 15.

Chapter 9
1. Collins, *Good to Great*, 18.

Chapter 10
1. Bass, Stanley. *Dr. Herbert Shelton: How Diseases Are Cured.* http://drbass.com/disease-cure.html (accessed January 18, 2008).

2. Chopra, Deepak. *Perfect Health: The Complete Mind/Body Guide (audiotape)* (New York: Simon & Schuster, 1995).

3. Mayoclinic.com. "Positive Thinking: Practice This Stress Management Skill." May 31, 2007. http://www.mayoclinic.com/health/positive-thinking/SR00009 (accessed February 7, 2008).

Chapter 12
1. Maslow, Abraham. "A Theory of Human Motivation," originally published in *Psychological Review* 50 (1943) 370–396. Quoted in *Journal of Advanced Hiring System*, October 17, 2006 http://www.advancedhiring.com/docs/theory_of_human_motivation.pdf (accessed February 7, 2008).

Chapter 14

1. Rogers, *On Becoming a Person,* 188.

2. Nemeth, *Mastering Life Energies,* 57.

3. Main, *The Heart of Creation,* 103.

4. Easwaren, *Meditation: A Simple Eight-Point Program,* 57–58.

Glossary

1. Flanagan, *Consciousness Reconsidered,* 99.

2. Carson & Buckist, *Psychology: The Science of Behavior,* 201.

Resources

Below is a brief, selected compilation of ongoing work done by various authors, organizations, and foundations in areas of interest related to this book. The resource material is useful for additional information and research. It is neither a complete list nor a "best of all" selection.

General Sites

- http://www.sma.org/pdfs/objecttypes/smj/36EC594F-BCD4-FF25-53BD223A47978F2D/00007611-200412000-00016.pdf

- http://www.hagelin.org/

- http://www.dalailamacenter.org/multimedia/index.php

- http://fcis.oise.utoronto.ca/~jmiller/

Education Resources

- http://www.wellesley.edu/RelLife/transformation/consultation.html

- http://www.wellesley.edu/RelLife/transformation/conhow-conceptpaper.html

- http://www.aplaceforpeace.org/UFBConferences.pdf click on A Unified Field-Based Approach to Education

- http://www.davidlynchfoundation.org/

- http://www.infed.org/biblio/holisticeducation.htm

- http://www.haven.net/edge/council/miller.htm

- http://members.iinet.net.au/~rstack1/world/papers/Education_Soul.doc

- http://www.ericdigests.org/2002-3/adult.htm

- http://www.kinfonet.org/Community/schools/Default.htm

Bibliography

Asher, James J. *Brainswitching: A Skill for the Twenty-first Century*. Los Gatos, CA: Sky Oaks, 1988.

Carson, N., and William Buckist. *Psychology: The Science of Behavior,* 5th ed. Needham Heights MA: Allyn & Bacon, 1997.

Byrne, Rhonda. *The Secret*. New York: Atria Books, 2006.

Canfield, Jack, and Mark Victor Hansen. *Chicken Soup for the Teacher's Soul*. Deerfield Beach, FL: Heath Communications Inc., 2002.

Chopra, Deepak. *The Seven Spiritual Laws of Success*. San Rafael, CA: New World Library, 1994.

Cloud, Henry. *Secret Things of God*. New York: Howard Books, 2007.

Collins, Jim. *Good to Great: Why Some Companies Make the Leap*. New York: Harper Collins, 2001.

Csikszentmihalyi, Mihaly. *Flow: The Psychology of Optimal Experience*. New York: Harper & Row Publishers, 1991.

deMello, Anthony. *Awareness: The Perils and Opportunities of Reality*. New York: Doubleday, 1990.

Easwaran, Eknath. *Meditation: A Simple Eight-Point Program for Translating Spiritual Ideals into Daily Life*. Tomales, CA: Nilgiri Press, 1991.

Ellis, Albert. *The Myth of Self-Esteem*. Amherst, NY: Prometheus Books, 2005.

Epstein, Mark. *Thoughts without a Thinker*. New York: Basic Books, 1995.

Flanagan, Owen. *Consciousness Reconsidered*. Cambridge, MA: Bradford Books, 1992.

Gratzon, Fred. *The Lazy Way to Success*. Fairfield, IA: Soma Press, 2003.

Helmsletter, Shad. *What to Say When You Talk to Yourself*. New York: Grindle Press, 1982.

Hicks, Esther, and Jerry Hicks. *The Amazing Power of Deliberate Intent*. Carlsbad, CA: Hay House Inc., 2006.

Krishnamurti, J. *The Ending of Time*. Brockwood Park, UK: First Harper & Row, 1985.

Krishnamurti, J. *The Awakening of Intelligence*. New York: Avon Books, 1976.

Krishnamurti, J. *Think on These Things*. New York: Perennial Library, 1970.

Levine, Stephen. *A Gradual Awakening*. New York: Doubleday Dell Publishing, 1989.

Lutyens, Mary, ed. *The Second Penguin Krishnamurti Reader*. Middlesex, England: Penguin Books, 1970.

Main, John. *The Heart of Creation*. London: Canterbury Press, 1977.

Main, John. *Silence and Stillness in Every Season: Daily Readings with John Main*. Edited by Paul Harris. New York: The Continuum International Publishing Group Inc., 1997.

Maslow, Abraham. *Toward a Psychology of Being*. New York: Wiley, 1998.

Maslow, Abraham. *Motivation and Personality*. New York: Addison-Wesley, 1987.

May, Rollo. *Man's Search for Himself*. New York: Dell Publishing, 1953.

Nemeth, Maria. *Mastering Life Energies*. Novato, CA: New World Library, 2007.

Oliner, Samuel P., and Pear M. Oliner. *The Altruistic Personality: Rescuers of Jews in Nazi Germany*. New York: The Free Press, 1988.

Papert, Seymour. *The Children's Machine*. New York: Basic Books, 1993.

Palmer, Parker. *The Courage to Teach*. San Francisco: Jossey-Bass Inc., 1998.

Postman, Neil, and Charles Weingartner. *Teaching as a Subversive Activity*. New York: Dell Publishing Co., 1969.

Rogers, Carl R. *On Becoming a Person*. New York: Houghton Mifflin, 1989.

Schucman, Helen, and William Thetford. *A Course in Miracles*. London: Penguin Books, 1976.

Tolle, Eckhart. *A New Earth*. London: Penguin Books, 2005.

Tolle, Eckhart. *The Power of Now*. Novato, CA: New World Library, 1999.

Tolle, Eckhart. *Stillness Speaks*. Vancouver, Canada: Namaste Publishing, 2003.

Trump, Donald. *Trump 101*. Hoboken, NJ: John Wiley & Sons, 2007.

Wilbur, Ken. *Sex, Ecology, Spirituality*. Boston: Shambhala Publications, Inc., 1995.

Printed in the United States
136012LV00005B/4/P